Presented to guests at
the dinner to celebrate
the Charter Anniversary
of the Rotary Club of
Stretford and Urmston;
March 23rd 2005.

Barrie Watkins
Hon.Librarian, Lancashire CCC.

Peter Charles
President.

David O'Hara
Hon. Secretary.

ARCHIE'S LAST STAND

M.C.C.
IN NEW ZEALAND
1922-23

ARCHIE'S LAST STAND

M.C.C.
IN NEW ZEALAND
1922-23

Being an Account of Mr A. C. MacLaren's Tour
and His Last Stand

by
DAVID KYNASTON

QUEEN ANNE PRESS
MACDONALD & CO
LONDON & SYDNEY

A QUEEN ANNE PRESS BOOK

© David Kynaston

First published in Great Britain in 1984 by
Queen Anne Press, Macdonald & Co (Publishers) Ltd,
Maxwell House, 74 Worship Street,
London EC2A 2EN

A BPCC plc company

Kynaston, David
ARCHIE'S LAST STAND
1. Marylebone Cricket Club—History
2. Cricket—New Zealand—History—20th century
I. Title
796.35'865   GV928.N45

ISBN 0-356-10548-2

The photographs on pages 51, 55, 67, 88, 112 are from the
Auckland Weekly News; those on pages 48, 60, 82, 121 are
from the *New Zealand Free Lance*, and are reproduced with
permission of The Alexander Turnbull Library, New Zealand.
The photographs on pages 30, 35, 38, 40, 59, 62, 74, 76, 92, 97, 98, 102, 111,
118, 132, 134, 142 are taken from the tour album of F. S. G. Calthorpe.
We are grateful to his widow, Mrs Dorothy Dury, for permission to
reproduce them.

Typeset by Cylinder Typesetting Ltd, London

Reproduced, printed and bound in Great Britain by
Hazell, Watson & Viney Limited,
Member of the BPCC Group
Aylesbury, Bucks

To Lucy
(in the far pavilion)

·PREFACE·

Cricket in New Zealand dates back at least to 1835, when Charles Darwin, during the voyage of the *Beagle*, watched farm workers at Waimate, on a property owned by British missionaries, playing a game in the evening. 'Very merry and good-humoured' was how he found them. Five years later, at the Treaty of Waitangi, New Zealand became a Crown Colony and the way was opened for a steady stream of British settlers, bringing their pastimes with them. One of the earliest matches with published scores was Nelson versus Surveyors of the New Zealand Land Company in 1844; but it was not until 1860, when an Auckland team arrived unannounced in Wellington, that the first representative contest was held. It was played at the Parade ground by Mount Cook's barracks, with the Basin Reserve, transformed by the great earthquake of 1855 from a lake into a swamp, not yet drained into a cricket ground. Soon, though, the Basin would take on its 'historic' character and eventually become the setting for further seismic experiences in, for example, 1922 and 1978.

The detailed study of New Zealand's cricket history has remained, since those pioneering days, a thing of fits and starts. Between the world wars, T. W. Reese's massive two volumes provided invaluable basic information about the earliest matches onwards, but comprised score-cards rather than continuous prose. Subsequently, Arthur Carman until recently kept the statistical tradition going with notable perseverance and accuracy. And more locally, R. T. Brittenden and Don Neely have written good narratives of cricket in Canterbury and Wellington respectively. An enormous amount, however, remains to be unearthed, mostly hidden away in local newspapers that are

6

often now defunct. It is these papers that provide the basis for this book and from which almost all unattributed quotations are derived. A full list is contained in the bibliography.

For their help in the research and writing of this particular slice of history, I would especially like to thank: R. W. Archer, Mildred Cambridge, John Carrad, Beet Chapman, Tim Curtis, Graham Dowling, Dorothy Dury, Iain Galloway, Alan Gibson, Jack Gregg, George Griffiths, Herb Lambert, Kate Lowe, Margot Lowry, John Maclean, Eddie McLeod, Don Neely, Grant Nisbett, Vincent O'Sullivan, Donald Peck, Terry Power, Max Reese, Dorothy Ricketts, Joseph Romanos, Wallace Smith, Colin Snedden, Mike Vockins, and the late Alex Wilkinson. In addition, Michael Down, author of an excellent recent biography of Archie MacLaren, replied encouragingly when I told him what I was doing. Harry and Rita Ricketts were staunch friends during my time in Wellington; while Max reminded me that present-day cricket also has its magic.

New Zealand

Pacific Ocean

Auckland

NORTH
ISLAND

Rotorua

New Plymouth

Napier

Wanganui

Marton
Palmerston
North

*Tasman
Sea*

Wellington

Nelson
Blenheim

Greymouth

Christchurch
Lyttleton

Geraldine

Temuka
Timaru

SOUTH

ISLAND

Queenstown

Lumsden

Dunedin

Invercargill

0   100   200 km

·1·

*Cricket's first World Cup — Pooley strikes trouble —
'Well bowled, Bos' — a googely is born — picquet on
deck — Hiddleston befriended — disappointing day
for South Canterbury attack*

The man who brought international cricket to New Zealand
was the Dunedin entrepreneur Dr Shadrach Jones, who in 1864
persuaded George Parr's English touring team to leave Australia
and participate in his Grand Tourney. Organised cricket in
New Zealand was only twenty spasmodic years old; the other
teams involved were Canterbury, Southland, and the home
province of Otago, and local interest was naturally keen. Otago
won both the domestic contests – 'luck was decidedly against
the Canterbury team, and it is pleasant to add that they bore
their reverses most good-naturedly' – but the real enthusiasm
was reserved for Parr's men, all professionals with the exception
of E. M. Grace. After the processions and dinners and firing of
guns, the cricket was inevitably rather anti-climactic, not helped
by gale conditions. Even though George Tarrant was debarred
from bowling his fast ones on account of the badness of the
wicket, Twenty-Two of Otago could muster only 71 and 83,
losing to the All England Eleven by nine wickets. There followed
a drawn match with Twenty-Two of Canterbury and Otago,
Grace top scoring for the third innings in succession, before the
tourists set out for Christchurch to play Canterbury alone.
Partly because of the elements, but partly also because 'the hill

9

facing the Grand Stand was much patronised by a class of people who could have well afforded the admission money to the ground', Jones had lost on his venture. A man indeed ahead of his time, because it was to be at least another century before cricket in New Zealand became anything like a money-spinner.

The match in Christchurch was commemorated by Samuel Butler, then making his living as a sheep-breeder in the Rangitata district. Not renowned as a cricket lover, he presumably had nowhere else to go. He sent the following verses to the local *Press:*

Claud: Which side went in first?
Hor: We did;
    And scored a paltry thirty runs in all.
    The lissom Lockyer gambolled round the stumps
    With many a crafty curvet: you had thought
    An Indian rubber were endued
    With wicket keeping instincts: teazing Tinley
    Issued his treacherous notices to quit
    Ruthlessly truthful to his fame, and who
    Shall speak of Jackson? Oh, 'twas sad indeed
    To watch the downcast faces of our men
    Returning from the wickets; one by one
    Like patients at the gratis consultation
    Of some skilled leech, they took their turn at physic,
    And each came sadly homeward with a face
    Awry through inward anguish; they were pale
    As ghosts of some dead but deep mourned love
    Grim with a great despair, but forced to smile.
Claud: Poor souls! Th' unkindest heart had bled for them.
    But what came after?
Hor: Fortune turned her wheel
    And Grace disgraced for the nonce was bowled
    First ball, and all the welkin roared applause.
    As for the rest they scored a goodly score
    And showed some splendid cricket, but their deeds
    Were not colossal, and our own brave Tennant
    Proved himself all as good a man as they.

More prosaically summarised, Canterbury's Twenty-Two collapsed for 30 to the lobs of 'Spider' Tinley, whose 13 wickets cost 18 runs; Parr's team replied with 137; and Canterbury in their second innings totalled 105, with A. E. Tennant scoring 28 and Tinley turning in the rather inflationary figures of 12 for 68. For a young settlement, drawing its players mainly from the top end of local society, it was a fairly honourable defeat.

The settlement was as old again when in 1877 the next English team visited Christchurch. James Lillywhite's party played matches at Auckland, Wellington, and New Plymouth before coming to South Island, where two fixtures preceded the one against Eighteen of Canterbury. On the morning of that match, the *Press* noted of the tourists' wicket-keeper: 'Pooley, who hurt his knee in Nelson, came on to Christchurch, instead of going to Greymouth, and has been up to the ground two or three times. He is very anxious to have the wicket well watered, but our committee do not quite see any reason why water should be put on, especially as it is well known that Shaw is perfectly unplayable on a dead wicket . . . . We have no doubt that Pooley perfectly understands this fact.' Not going to Greymouth turned out to be the best thing that happened to Ed Pooley in South Island, because the rest of the team arrived forty eight hours later in Christchurch, only just in time for the match, desperately stiff, cold, and weary after a nightmarish journey in which they had been almost drowned in their coach trying to cross the swollen Otira River. Eventually, 'shortly before one o'clock, Fowler and Lillywhite tossed up for choice of innings. The latter won, and with a smile of pleasure remarked, "We go in".' It would have been an unpopular toss to lose, though in fact only a last-wicket stand between Hill and Southerton took the score from 39 for 9 up to a total of 70. Canterbury at stumps were 27 for 4 (no ducks). One of the umpires on that first day was Pooley, but during the second he had to be relieved because his knee flared up again. The final scores of the three-day match were England 70 and 102, Canterbury 65 (four ducks, none of them leg-before) and 84 (seven ducks), with Alfred Shaw unable to bowl in the home team's second innings.

Two days later the tourists were facing Eighteen of Otago at Dunedin, where 'the Eleven occupied their usual places in the field, except that Pooley took short leg, having received an accident to his eye in Christchurch, and Jupp occupied his post at the wickets'. Midway through Otago's second innings, however, 'amid general cheering', Pooley took up his usual position and proceeded to make two smart stumpings off Lillywhite. That final day was memorable indeed, as Otago, 86 to England's 163 in the first innings, battled to save the match: 'After lunch the attendance was very numerous, increasing hourly, until at five o'clock there must have been fully 4,000 within the enclosure. The finish was most exciting. There was extensive betting on a one innings defeat.' And presumably also against such a defeat, for with Otago's score at 76 for 16, 'several gentlemen then surrounded Collinson, who, on account of a bad leg, had not intended to go in, and persuaded him to take his stand at the wickets with the hopes of Nicholls being able to make the necessary run. This he did in his ordinary dress, without pads or gloves, and got through the rest of Lillywhite's over successfully.' In the end they put on 20, Collinson 2 not out, and, with only five minutes of playing time left, the match was drawn. At that point Pooley walked off the field to find himself arrested, leaving the rest of the team to entrain that evening for Invercargill, where they met Southland, and then to return to Melbourne, where, still without him, they played what turned out to be the first Test match between England and Australia.

Pooley instead (in the company of the team's baggage man and money-taker, Alf Bramall) was in the magistrate's court at Christchurch, accused of having, in the billiard room bar of the Commercial Hotel, assaulted one Ralph Donkin, a resident of Warner's Hotel, which was also in Christchurch. The trouble stemmed, as Pooley explained to the court, from a bet which he had struck several days before the Canterbury match one evening at Warner's Hotel, where the local selection committee had posted the list of the side to meet the English: 'Donkin laid him six pounds to one pound that he (Pooley) did not name the individual score of the Eighteen. Witness asked Donkin for the money, and some high words ensued in the hotel, and witness struck him slightly. In the street, witness again asked Donkin for the money, and he turned round and struck witness with his stick, and then witness closed with him in self-defence . . . . When witness named the individual score of each of the Eighteen, he put down a number against each name. The number he put down was 0.' It was an old, old trick of touring professionals, worth in this case thirty six pounds according to Pooley's calculations, but in the vehement view of Donkin a 'catch' bet which he refused to pay. Who had really struck whom first and hardest on the evening the match ended is impossible to say, but in the event Pooley on his assault charge was fined five pounds and costs. He had also, however, to face a charge of wilful and malicious damage to personal property, worth some ninety eight pounds. The scenario in this case was that Donkin, a surveyor in his professional life, was advised after the fracas to leave his hotel for that night, after it had been relayed to him that Pooley was threatening to 'pay the **** out before the night was over'; and that when he returned to his hotel room the following morning, some of his clothes had been torn and various tracings and plans of the Lyttelton waterworks burnt. The case against Pooley and Bramall was adjourned for several weeks, when the supreme court found them not guilty, presumably on the grounds of lack of hard evidence. Pooley then made his own way back to England, solaced, according to one account, by the subscription raised on his behalf by a section of the Christchurch public who felt he had had a raw deal. Six more years of professional cricket for Surrey lay ahead of him, followed by poverty and the workhouse, before he died at Lambeth Infirmary in 1907.

New Zealand cricket for the rest of the century continued its uphill struggle against lack of money, lack of a leisured class, lack of population generally, and (especially in Wellington) lack of playing grounds, an array of handicaps compounded by geographical isolation. The Maori remained indifferent and rugby increasingly dominated the national sporting consciousness. English teams called in to play matches in 1879, 1882 (William Midwinter 78 wickets at 3.1 each), and 1888, but the almost invariably one-sided games that took place were entirely subservient to the main purpose of touring Australia. By contrast, visiting Australian teams, though mostly going to or from England, proliferated in this period, culminating in 1894 when the first national side was assembled for the purpose of playing New South Wales. That same year saw the formation of the New Zealand Cricket Council. Tours abroad remained a rarity, perhaps because of the experience in 1878-79 of the Canterbury Eleven in Victoria, which found itself in the state at the same time as an English party and consequently proved such a poor draw that it required money sent from Christchurch to pay for the team's voyage home. In 1898-99, however, a national team of sorts was sent to Australia, where unfortunately, in the words of T. W. Reese, 'the peculiar atmosphere and tall buildings in Melbourne and Sydney affected many of the players'. There was still no question of anything even remotely approaching parity with either England or Australia: for instance, when the Australians visited in 1897-98, New Zealand in the 'Test' match (as her representative contests were being called by then, though official status was still a long way off) put fifteen players into the field. Domestically, though, things *were* perceptibly improving, helped especially by the spread of railways in the 1880s and importation of professional coaches from 1890. Otago, Canterbury, and Wellington played regularly against each other, with Canterbury tending to have the edge, while Auckland was still relatively inaccessible until the main trunk line was completed in 1908. At club level, matches were organised on the distinctive basis of being played over two consecutive (when possible) Saturday afternoons, one new ball lasting an afternoon. A week could be a long time in such cricket: on 15 November 1884, George Watson, captain of the Midland club in Christchurch and scorer of the first first-class century in New Zealand, was not out 4 at close of play, but 'absent' on the 22nd, dead on the 23rd.

It was in 1902-3 that an English team at last arrived to make a full tour, with the specific purpose of encouraging cricket in the country at large. In the last-minute absence of Lord Hawke, captain of the side was Pelham Warner, who led a strongish party (perhaps average county) comprising mainly amateurs, though with two professionals, George Thompson of Northants and Sam Hargreave of Warwicks. The New Zealand Cricket Council organised the tour, paying the amateurs their travelling and hotel expenses, minus their wine and washing bills. The two professionals received a lump sum in addition to all expenses bar their wine bills. As much as possible, the Council sought to cut down on hotel expenses by billeting the amateurs privately. Thus when the team arrived at Dunedin, the *Otago Witness* reported that 'Mr Warner is staying with Dr Lindo

Ferguson, Mr Whatman with Mr James Mills, Messrs Dowson and Bosanquet with Mr John Roberts, Messrs Stanning and Fane at the Fernhill Club, and Messrs Hargreave and Thompson at the City Hotel'. This plan had its obvious financial attractions (the tour made a profit), but the general feeling amongst New Zealand cricketers was quite strongly that their own social intercourse with the visitors was being cut off to the detriment of the tour's overall purpose. Such certainly was the view of Dan Reese, the Canterbury all-rounder who emerged during this tour as an outstanding cricketer. But as he also went on in his notably well-written and instructive memoirs, *Was It All Cricket?* (1948), 'the way this team stalked through the Dominion, demonstrating the correctness and efficiency of the Englishman's style of play, is still talked of today'. For the first time a big-match atmosphere came to New Zealand: the outlying districts proved no contest for the visitors, but in both Wellington and Christchurch five-figure crowds saw the local province putting up a good fight, in Wellington's case amply justifying the decision, reached after agonising debate, to play with eleven men rather than fifteen. Two 'Tests' were played, New Zealand losing the first a little unluckily, the second soundly. And in Warner's considered opinion, 'there was some friction, but the tour was, on the whole, a great success'.

The local difficulty that Warner had in mind was no doubt the 'incident' that took place at Christchurch as Canterbury, on 28 for 0, chased an implausible 288 to win. The *Lyttelton Times* related the version of one of the participants:

Mr R. Spencer, who was umpiring at square-leg, states that Bosanquet was bowling to Pearce. He appeared to pitch a ball well to leg, and Pearce turned to play it hard to square-leg. Thinking that the ball was coming in his direction, Mr Spencer half turned to dodge it, and on recovering his position he found that one of Pearce's bails had been dislodged. Pearce appeared inclined to leave his crease, one or more of the players having called out 'Well bowled, Bos', but Sims [the non-striker] called to the batsman to appeal. Pearce thereupon appealed to Bannerman [Charles Bannerman, the old Australian batsman, then coaching at Christ's College in Christchurch], at whose end the decision rested, and Bannerman stated that he had not seen what happened and, therefore, appealed to Spencer, who stated

15

that he could not give a decision . . . . Bannerman was again appealed to, and reiterated that he had not seen what happened. The Englishmen then appealed again to Spencer, who declined once more to give a decision. There was some argument, and ultimately the game proceeded. Spencer states that subsequently he heard the wicketkeeper, Whatman, addressing comments to Sims, the purport of which he could not catch.

In fact, Whatman accused Sims of being a cheat even to query that Pearce had been bowled; while Warner apparently called it the 'most disgraceful decision he had ever heard in the field'. It was clear that the episode thoroughly rattled the batsmen. 'The following ball was hit high to the off by Pearce, but Dowson missed taking the catch'; Sims was soon bowled for 8 'running out to Bosanquet'; and Pearce was stumped by Whatman off the same bowler. Canterbury then gently subsided to 154 all out, but the fury of the local press the next day was intense, condemning the English players not only for openly disputing the umpires' decision ('If Canterbury men had done such a thing, "shockingly bad form" would be the mildest comment to expect from University-trained players'), but also for getting at Sims ('a highly-strung boy only just out of his teens') and, indirectly, Pearce. Warner subsequently apologised for the incident on behalf of his team, but feelings still ran so high that Arthur Sims was told by his employers, the Canterbury Frozen Meat Company, that unless he received a personal apology from Whatman, he would not be given any further leave of absence to play against the tourists. This Whatman apparently failed to do, for in the ensuing 'Test', Sims, though selected, stood down from the New Zealand team.

On the technical front, the New Zealanders were fascinated by 'Boosanky', as they called him, and his pioneering form of spin-bowling, which he had first demonstrated in public in 1900 for Middlesex against Leicestershire. The various press accounts, taken together, give some idea of what it was like. The first match was at Auckland, where Bosanquet 'placed four men in the country, and then sent up slows with a big break, at which the local men were completely at sea'. While according to another paper, 'Bosanquet can bowl to order, either a fastish, bumpy ball, or slow leg and off lobs. For the latter he has seven of his field placed on the leg side, and delivers well to that side, some of his balls being almost out of reach.' Bosanquet's figures in this match were not all that startling, but at Wanganui a couple of weeks later he took 6 for 18 in the local team's second innings and prompted the *Wanganui Herald* to comment: 'Bosanquet, the slow bowler, proved very puzzling to the local batsmen. His delivery appears to be ridiculously easy and slow, but the break is phenomenal from either side, and the batsman cannot tell from his delivery whether the break will be from leg or off.' A few days later, at Palmerston North, Cooke in Manawatu's second innings 'was batting very confidently until Bosanquet beat him with a trick ball', which 'had a phenomenal break from leg, and came in right behind the batsman'. And in general, according to the *Manawatu Evening Standard*, 'his slow deliveries were very akin to jugglery, and the local batsmen knew nothing at all about them'. What, then, is one to make of this 'slow bowler, who bowled round the wicket, going only two paces before delivering the ball'? Perhaps the leg-break remained his staple slow ball, while the one that without apparent change of action went the other way he still bowled only relatively occasionally, though with considerable if sometimes inaccurate purchase. But what to call it? The great linguistic break-through occurred at Wellington, where, reporting Wellington's second innings, the *New Zealand Times* for January 19 referred to how 'Bosanquet's "googely ones" were relished by the batsmen, and in one over he was banged for 11'. That paper's cricket correspondent may not have actually coined the term, but it does seem to have been the first written usage. Warner in his tour book, published soon afterwards, referred to 'Bosanquet's slow "googlies"' as 'as they were called in New Zealand'. But as to *why* they were called so, it is difficult to go beyond Warner's own suggestion that 'the word meant something weird, freakish, almost uncanny'.

Four seasons later, in 1906, the first official MCC team to tour New Zealand set out on board the S.S. *Corinthic*. It was an all-amateur affair, captained by E. G. Wynyard and including Johnny Douglas and the well-known 'lobster' G. H. T. Simpson-Hayward. Also on that voyage out was Katherine Mansfield, just eighteen and now returning to her family home in Wellington after three years at Queen's College in Harley Street. In the course of the journey she developed a truly teenage crush on one of the cricketers:

R is my latest. The first time I saw him I was lying back in my chair, and he walked past. I watched the complete rhythmic movement, the absolute self-confidence, the beauty of his body . . . . I heard him speaking: he has a low, full, strangely exciting voice, a habit of mimicking others, a keen sense of humour. His face is clean cut, like the face of a statue, his mouth absolutely Grecian. Also he has seen much and lived much and his hand is perfectly strong and cool. He is certainly tall, and his clothes shape the lines of his figure. When I am with him a preposterous desire seizes me, I want to be badly hurt by him. I should like to be strangled by his firm hands. He smokes cigarettes frequently and exquisitely fastidiously.

Last night we sat on deck. He taught me picquet. It was intensely hot. He wore a loose silk shirt under his dress coat. He was curiously excitable, almost a little violent at times. There was a suppressed agitation in every look, every movement. He spoke French for the greater part of the time with exquisite fluency and a certain extreme affectation. He has spent years in Paris. The more hearts you have the better, he said, leaning over my hand . . . .

Yesterday afternoon a game of cricket was in progress on the deck. He began bowling. I stood and watched. He took a few slow steps, and then flung the ball at the wicket with the most marvellous force. But every time he did it, each ball seemed to be aimed at my heart.

Who is 'R'? Assuming that really is his initial, the only moderately convincing candidate is R. H. (Ronny) Fox, who had been in the Haileybury Eleven in 1898 and otherwise had confined his significant cricket to a handful of appearances for the MCC during the mid-1900s. In the ship's fancy dress ball he went as a Maori chief, conceivably as a result of Katherine's enthusiasm for the natives, though he himself was a New Zealander by birth. One problem is that Fox was the team's wicket-keeper, though against Fifteen of Wairarapa at Masterton, he did take 5 for 10 and 3 for 14, bowling medium pace with considerable swerve. A more serious difficulty is that at least sometimes he wore a moustache, though a fairly small one. In purely physical terms, a likely contender is surely Douglas, at that time as celebrated a boxer as he was a cricketer; while to judge by the description of the bowling, it seems, regretfully, that Simpson-Hayward is out of the running.

The romance failed to blossom once the team reached New Zealand and the strenuous travelling and semi-serious cricket got under way. 'The English cricket team are all perfectly charming and it is just lovely when they are in Wellington', wrote Katherine's sister, Chaddie, after a dance given for the team, but there is no evidence that Katherine herself continued any liaison.[1] Wellington in fact proved an unlucky place for what was a fairly patchy team: against Wellington itself Wynyard broke a tendon and had to return to England, with C. E. de Trafford taking over as captain; while in the second of the two 'Tests', the visitors, having won the first, succumbed to some fine quick bowling from the local player Ernest Upham. They also lost to Canterbury, but otherwise had a reasonably comfortable time. Crowds were on the whole poor and the tour made a substantial loss, which was borne by the New Zealand Cricket Council and no doubt explains why there were no more MCC tours to the Dominion before the war. There may also have been a certain undertow of resentment at the rather lordly ways of the mostly very young amateurs, to judge by the tone as well as content of a story that appeared in Wellington's illus-trated social weekly, the *New Zealand Free Lance:*

When the British cricket team arrived from the south at Wellington, some of them chartered a cab to drive them to the hotel. They had arranged that the fare should be five shillings, and on arrival at the hotel they paid. But the cabman remarked that there was sixpence wharfage. This, of course, seemed preposterous, don't you know, and a long, earnest conference happened. Then, with some circumstance, one cricketer produced a threepenny and tendered it. The cabbie took it and remarked: "No, no! I wants me sprat!"

Another cricketer searched ardently in his pockets and produced a sixpence. "Heah, me man, is a bally sixpence! You have ninepence now. Quite a bonus for a person of your rank!" he remarked. "'Ere,

[1]. A few months later she wrote in her journal, reviewing her emotional life, 'I have been foolish many times (especially with Oscar Fox).' Whether 'Oscar' was a nickname is uncertain.

take yer thrum, sonnie!" replied the cabbie, "I wouldn't rob yer!" The cricketer threw the coin at him violently. A porter picked it up. "I'll punch a hole in it", he said, "and hang it on me watchchain as a sooveener of the visit of these bloomin' English cricketers!"

A few weeks later, however, the same paper had a more flattering item about the visitors: 'Every time a fieldsman missed a ball or dropped a catch he apologised to the bowler, and whenever a fieldsman did a fine piece of work all his fellows would give a small bit of applause to him. The latter was a pretty action and could well be copied by local players.' Clearly, there remained a certain rough-and-readiness about New Zealand cricket as well as society that was not altogether in accordance with the *mores* of tall young men with Grecian mouths and loose silk shirts.

Probably of more help than tours to the country's cricketing progress during the 1900s was that two top-flight English professionals played for and coached particular provinces. In the mid-1900s the old Notts fast bowler Frank Shacklock (from whose name Conan Doyle reputedly derived that of his hero) was a powerful presence in Otago cricket, using the time-honoured English method of leg-ropes to stop back feet from sliding away; while later in the decade the Sussex all-rounder Albert Relf, stressing the virtues of patience and orthodoxy, personally welded Auckland together into a formidable outfit. Domestic competition was further sharpened with the establishment in 1906 of the Plunket Shield, which up to the war was played on a challenge basis and was held by either Auckland or Canterbury. It would be a frustrating system. In 1908 the visiting Otago captain, C.G.Wilson, persuaded Auckland's captain to agree to play the challenge match to a finish, and then proceeded to score 144 himself on the first day; but after the third day, with Otago in a winning position, Auckland successfully invoked the existing three-day agreement made by the provincial cricket associations, leaving the match drawn and Otago to travel back home empty-handed. 'Gillie' Wilson (later known as 'Father') was a forceful Australian who had played for Victoria before moving to Invercargill in 1902 to manage the branch there of the soft goods firm of Sargood, Son, and Ewen. He at once assumed the captaincy of Southland, until business took him in 1906 to Dunedin and then in 1912 to Wellington. At Invercargill he took under his wing a promising young batsman called Sid Hiddleston and gave him a job, though Hiddleston was still only a boy, in the firm. Thereafter, wherever Wilson went his protégé followed, making his Plunket Shield debut for Otago and later shining for Wellington in the two seasons before the war. Alongside Hiddleston in that Wellington team was Clarrie Grimmett, who took 22 first-class wickets at 31 each before, in 1914, the province's Australian coach, J. V. Saunders, successfully convinced him that the best place for his leg-breaks was the land of harder wickets across the Tasman. The besetting problem for New Zealand cricket as a whole, though, was not emigration but money. When the Canterbury team made a successful challenge at Auckland in 1911, only a public subscription got them there in the first place. And when in 1913 a New Zealand team was sent to Australia, performing reasonably well, the NZCC was only able to reimburse the players five shillings a day in lieu of wages, which was hardly adequate.

Yet later in that 1913-14 season all financial cares were forgotten as Arthur Sims, by now based in Melbourne and a prosperous frozen meat exporter in his own right, brought over a glittering team of Australians for a series of what turned into virtually exhibition matches. Appropriately it was in his home city of Christchurch that Sims put on 433 for the eighth wicket with Victor Trumper, whose 293 was described by T. W. Reese in 1927 as 'the greatest innings ever seen in the Dominion'. Canterbury's stock bowler, J. H. Bennett, was convinced that he had Trumper caught behind for 7, but in the end it was Don Sandman who took the catch to dismiss him 'at cover point as it came down from the skies'. Sims's team, winning by an innings and 364 runs, then travelled to Temuka to play South Canterbury, where at least one paper, the *Timaru Herald*, was quietly confident that the local men 'should be able to give a good account of themselves and, whatever happens, they can hardly fare worse than the Canterbury team which was so soundly beaten yesterday'. The story of the two-day match is well-known: South Canterbury (batting with fifteen men, but fielding eleven) scored 180 and the Australians at stumps were 117 for 3;

21

this score advanced by the end of the second day to 922 for 9, with the former Surrey player J.N. Crawford scoring 354 in about four hours, though no satisfactory record exists of the exact time. In sixty nine minutes he added 298 with Trumper (135), in nine minutes the final 50 with Monty Noble. It was an astonishing display of hitting, though it is true that in the 290s he, in the unabashed words of the *Timaru Herald*, 'steadied up a bit, having displayed a certain amount of recklessness earlier in the game'. That day was undoubtedly a highlight of the tour, though about a week later Trumper scored a rapid 211 against Southland. The final match was played against New Zealand on the new Eden Park ground in Auckland. The *New Zealand Observer* described Trumper's batting as the Australians rattled up 610 for 6 declared: 'Though not timing too well he gave a great exhibition of hitting. He must have scored his last 60 runs at a great pace. Included in his score were four beautiful sixes, made without any undue effort.' On 81 he fell leg-before to Nesbit Snedden: it was the last first-class innings of his life, after a few short weeks in which he had brought something of the 'Golden Age' to New Zealand cricket.

·2·

*MacLaren in demand — a gallery of amateurs —
white heather at St Pancras — Wilson takes a dip —
Swan fails to score — an old master returns — a local
shower — Brice warms up — Kortlang breezes in —
strike-bound!*

There was talk of an MCC team under Kent's Lionel Trough-
ton touring New Zealand in 1920-21, but it came to nothing.
Instead, Vernon Ransford took over a team of young Australians; they played attractive cricket and the tour was an almost
complete success, marred only by disappointing attendances
for the 'Test' at Auckland. A few months later the MCC tried to
get together another amateur team, which would tour New
Zealand in 1921-22 and also play some matches in Australia,
part of the profits of which would go to the New Zealand Cricket
Council, in turn responsible for meeting all expenses.
The probable line-up received a dusty, cabled response
from the NZCC in Christchurch: 'TEAM AS SUBMITTED
NOT SUFFICIENTLY PROMINENT ENSURE GOOD
RESULT AUSTRALIA WHICH IS ESSENTIAL FOR
FINANCE CANNOT YOU POSSIBLY SECURE TENNY-
SON GILLINGHAM SPOONER BETTINGTON OR SOME
PLAYERS WHO HAVE REPRESENTED ENGLAND.' But
Lord's failed to produce the stars and the NZCC withdrew its
invitation, leading to a fairly acrimonious letter from Lord
Harris to Lord Jellicoe, then Governor-General in New Zealand.

Finally, however, the following year, both ends got their acts together and it was arranged to send an MCC team in the winter of 1922-23 under the captaincy of A. C. MacLaren, who had suggested himself to the NZCC as early as September 1921 and whose name alone was guarantee of at least fair gates in Australia. Originally, MacLaren had proposed the tour as a private venture, paying expenses and taking half the gate money, which was apparently acceptable to the NZCC, but not to the MCC. Instead, it was mutually agreed that the NZCC would receive any profit the tour made, including seventy five per cent of net profits from the matches played in Australia against the various states; that the NZCC would be responsible for all travel and hotel costs; and that if the tour made an overall loss, the MCC would meet half of it. It was a generous arrangement on the part of the MCC (not to mention the Australian authorities), induced no doubt by a missionary wish to improve the state of New Zealand cricket, but perhaps also prompted by a sense of guilt arising from the fact that a stronger, more 'bankable' English team was to be sent at the same time to tour South Africa.

Acting on the NZCC's behalf in London during the negotiations were the New Zealand statesman Sir Francis Bell and the Essex chairman H. D. Swan, who had recently agreed to become the Council's English representative. The basic terms were reached in May 1922, but by the end of the month there was a note of exasperation in Bell's latest cable back: 'MACLAREN REQUIRES EXPENSES HIS WIFE ACCOMPANYING HIM TO BE INCLUDED IN GROSS EXPENSES DOES COUNCIL AGREE IMMEDIATE REPLY IS REQUESTED STOP NEITHER SWAN NOR MYSELF HAVE BEEN ABLE TO SEE MACLAREN HIM-SELF OR OBTAIN DETAILS LORDS COMMITTEE EQUALLY IN DARK CANNOT ASCERTAIN WHAT ARRANGEMENTS IF ANY MACLAREN HAS MADE OR NAMES OF PLAYERS HE PROPOSES BRINGING.' The NZCC replied thus early in June: 'MOST RELUCTANT ESTABLISH PRECEDENT MRS MACLAREN BUT WE MUST HAVE MACLAREN AND WE WILL CONSENT IF THERE IS NO ALTERNATIVE.'

Why was Archie MacLaren's participation on the tour so desirable? By 1922 he was fifty years old; it was over a quarter of a century since he had established what was still a world first-class record by scoring 424 for Lancashire against Somerset; he had not scored a first-class century since 1910, and since the war he had played only three first-class innings. Yet he still retained what H.S.Altham once called that 'general air of procunsular authority', an air that throughout his career informed every activity of MacLaren, but above all at the batting crease. 'He didn't merely hook the ball, he dismissed it from his presence', wrote Neville Cardus in one of the great snapshots of cricket writing. And indeed, though often remembered through various photographs for the boldness of his driving, it was even more MacLaren's hook and pull strokes that made him the formidable batsman he was. For an overall impression of that unique presence, C.B.Fry's oft-quoted description is worth quoting again: 'He lifted his bat for his stroke round his neck like a golfer at the top of his full swing. He stood bolt upright and swept into every stroke, even a defensive backstroke, with deliberate and dominating completeness. He never hedged on his stroke; he never pulled his punches.' MacLaren's greatest batting performances had tended to be in Australia, which he had toured three times (1894-95, 1897-98, 1901-2), scoring four of his five Test centuries there, including two at Sydney. And his reputation in that country was enormous, as the old Australian batsman John Worrall recalled in 1922 at the time of MacLaren's return: 'No English captain who has visited Australia has been as well liked by our own cricketers .... What particularly appealed to all of us who came into close touch with the Scotch-Lancastrian was that in many of his ways and in certain of his sayings – as he was at times rather free of speech – he more nearly approached our standards than any other English captain in my time .... In common with Australian cricketers, he played to win, and always fairly. For his keenness, judgement, sporting qualities, and batting skill, all old Australian Test players especially have an abiding admiration for MacLaren.'

Yet the fact was that between 1897-98 and 1909, captaining England for most of that time, MacLaren's record as a leader had been notably poor, never winning a rubber and only occasionally a Test. There was no denying, especially by MacLaren himself, that he had had many strokes of ill fortune during that tenure, but an equally valid clue to the string of failures perhaps lies in a story, told by Dan Reese, about the time MacLaren and Hayward enjoyed a big opening partnership in 1901-2 against New South Wales: 'They had scored over 300 runs when Hayward was out to a bad stroke. He had just had his shower-bath when MacLaren, the next man out, bounced into the dressing-room. One would have expected a "Well played, Tom!" Instead, he said, "Why in the devil did you want to make a stroke like that?"' Reese himself admired MacLaren's captaincy ('I remember being impressed with the way MacLaren whipped his team along to victory', he wrote of a narrow Lancashire win in 1906) and there is little doubt that his strategic grasp was unrivalled amongst contemporaries. The failings were more in the sphere of man management; not only could he be too authoritarian, but he also, in Altham's apposite words, 'rather lacked the gift of making others believe in, and so make the best of, themselves'. In general, for all his conversational charm as well as impressive bearing, there were undeniable flaws in MacLaren the man, taking perhaps three main forms: a certain thin-skinned haughtiness, possibly derived from having a more mercantile background than he would have wished; a tactlessness in human relations that had the effect of consistently rubbing at least some people up the wrong way; and lastly, almost ubiquitously, an astonishing lack of scruples in financial matters. Maybe he was not quite a 'rogue', as he has sometimes been called, but he was hardly far from it.

There are some signs that by the early 1920s, in his relative old age, MacLaren was mellowing a little towards those who played under him. In the famous match at Eastbourne in August 1921, when his team inflicted the first defeat on Warwick Armstrong's Australians despite being bowled out for 43 in the first innings, he was full of paternal encouragement to his young players; and as coach the following season at Old Trafford, as well as captain of the second team, he was remembered in later years as a kindly influence. In fact, it is the triumph at Eastbourne that holds the key to why MacLaren was as keen as he was to have a final fling down under. Throughout the disastrous summer of 1921 he had loudly proclaimed that the England sides were far too reliant on elderly professionals who lacked the necessary élan and agility to put up a real fight; then at Eastbourne his chosen team of amateurs had won the match by brilliant fielding as much as anything else. Now, in the wake of that success, a tour of New Zealand and the Australian states seemed the best possible way of bringing some of his favoured young amateurs still further on, with the ultimate object of getting perhaps two or three of them on the boat for the next full-scale tour to Australia in 1924-25. However, the team he now took with him was not necessarily *quite* the team he would have chosen. For one thing, the tour to South Africa had priority – otherwise, MacLaren would almost certainly have taken Greville Stevens, possibly also Arthur Gilligan. For another thing, he was not the sole selector: the MCC had its say too, which meant that several of the players that went had never been seen in action before by their captain. What one can say, though, is that the strongly Varsity character of the team was fully in accordance with the precepts of MacLaren, who seems to have felt for Oxbridge cricketers a degree of respect attributable only to his own lack of a university education. The following, however chosen, were the eleven amateurs through whom MacLaren sought to rejuvenate the rather tired image of English cricket:

Lieut-Col J. C. HARTLEY (47) (Vice-captain): In cricketing terms an improbable choice, but presumably drafted in by the MCC to act as an 'establishment' antidote to MacLaren's vagaries. 'Jock' Hartley's finest hour on the cricket field had occurred in the Varsity match twenty six years earlier, finding a 'spot' with his slow to medium leg-breaks to such effect that he took 11 wickets in the defeat of Cambridge, including Jessop's twice. Son of E. F. Hartley of Burnley, Lancs; educated Tonbridge. Two earlier tours: with Frank Mitchell's amateur side to North America in 1895; and with the MCC to South Africa in 1905-6 when, in Warner's words, he 'was most effective against the weaker teams, but the higher class batsmen found no difficulty in jumping out and driving him'. Two Tests in South Africa: 15 runs at 3.75, one wicket for 115. Moderate batsman. Occasional appearances for Sussex, when military duties allowed. Queen's medal, five clasps, King's medal, two clasps, despatches in the South African war; D.S.O., twice wounded, despatches thrice in the Great War.

Hon D. F. BRAND (20): David Brand, son of third Viscount Hampden, was a late replacement for R. St. L. Fowler, who had been unable to obtain leave from the Army. Chosen on the recommendation of Lord Harris, after some good scores for the Eton Ramblers. Captain of Eton in 1921 and, according to *Wisden*, 'especially praised for his management of the bowling'. Played for Cambridge University versus the Army in 1922 (scoring 2 and taking one for 55); failed to get a Blue. 'Another medium-pace bowler, with all his cards on the table, and his best trump a nice length.' (Melbourne *Argus*.)

A. P. F. CHAPMAN (22): MacLaren was lucky indeed that Percy Chapman, rapidly emerging as the golden boy of his epoch, had not been selected to go to South Africa. In 1922 he followed a delightful century for Cambridge in the Varsity match with an innings of 160 for Gentlemen versus Players at Lord's that was, in the words of the *Sporting Life*, of 'superlative brilliance'. His school career at Oakham (200 retired against Stoneygate at the age of 13) and Uppingham had been equally glittering. In the Cambridge side for three years. Played for MacLaren's team at Eastbourne in 1921. Born in Berkshire, and still playing for that county while qualifying for Kent. Had emerged during the 1922 season as a cover point of thrilling speed and certainty. Tall, charming, and handsome, the world lay before him.

C. H. GIBSON (22): Glem Gibson had also played at Eastbourne, taking 6 for 64 in the Australians' second innings. Four years in the Eton eleven, two in the Cambridge, and a few appearances for Sussex. Elected Cambridge's secretary for 1922, but instead had returned 'for business reasons' to the Argentine, where his father, Sir Herbert Gibson, was a wealthy ranch-owner, fanatical pioneer of advanced sheep-breeding, and generally prominent figure. A useful batsman, but a genuinely top-flight bowler. 'With a good run-up and a beautifully easy action, he bowled fast-medium, kept at his best a good length and made the ball swing very late. His best one would pitch on the leg stump and hit the off.' (*Wisden.*) 'With his perfect action, peculiar flight, variations of pace and irreproachable length, he has everything that a high-class bowler should possess.' (MacLaren.) Always an elegant, immaculately turned-out figure.

Hon F.S.GOUGH-CALTHORPE (30): Freddie Calthorpe, son of eighth Baron Calthorpe, was in many ways an archetypal amateur of the time. 'Who will forget his jolly laugh? And what a beautiful dancer he was! It was a real pleasure to see him dancing with his charming wife who was equally good. He told me that one May week at Cambridge he must have danced thirty miles with her.' (Warner.) Calthorpe had been a Cambridge Blue for three years before the war and for one after, when only a misdirected letter had deprived him of the captaincy. After a few pre-war appearances for Sussex, he began playing for Warwickshire (where his family seat was) in 1919, captaining the side from 1920. Had no relish for fast bowling, but drove well and, according to *Wisden*, 'cut the short ball in true Repton style'. Bowling something above medium, he could swerve the new ball and also obtain late swing: 'the effortless grace of Calthorpe's curving run up to the crease was something quite unforgettable'. (Rowland Ryder.) In the Royal Flying Corps during the war, having transferred there from the Staffordshire Yeomanry. Shortly before the tour, he took 4 for 4 when Warwickshire bowled out Hampshire for 15 and still lost. A great trier.

W.W.HILL-WOOD (21): Although in the Eton eleven for three years and making intermittent appearances for Derbyshire since 1919, it had taken a well-nigh infamous innings at Lord's for Willie Hill-Wood to win notice. Opening the batting for Cambridge in the Varsity match in 1922, in front of a paying crowd of over 11,000, he scored 81 in 285 minutes, a 'monumentally patient but undistinguished innings' as one of the kinder critics put it. 'Adopting a crouching stance, with both knees bent, and his bat hidden behind his left leg, he watched the ball right on to his bat.' (*Sporting Life.*) Second son of the

'Willie'

well-known sportsman Samuel Hill-Wood, who had captained Derbyshire around the turn of the century while also nursing Glossop FC to league status. Red-haired, with a keen sense of humour.

T. C. LOWRY (24): A New Zealander, from Hawke's Bay, Tom Lowry was son of the owner of one of the biggest stations in the country. Coached as a boy by Jack 'Jump out and 'it it, sir!' Board, he had then gone to Christ's College in Christchurch and an aviation school near Auckland, for which province he made his first-class debut, as a wicket-keeper, in 1917-18. After the war, some big-game hunting in Africa. Debut for Somerset in 1921: residential qualification as 'born Wellington'. Pipped by Hill-Wood for last batting place in Cambridge eleven in 1922. 'A large, powerful man, he batted with a short back lift, but urged the ball in front of the wicket with massive thrusts and pushes.' (Ian Peebles.) According to Robertson-Glasgow, he batted for Somerset in an old Homburg hat. A positive, no-nonsense character.

J. F. MACLEAN (21): John Maclean had played only one season's first-class cricket before going on the tour. 'We have found a more than useful wicket-keeper in J. F. Maclean, and next year he ought to prove himself a good batsman when he has gained the necessary experience.' (Review of Worcestershire in 1922 in the *Cricketer*.) 'Played a capital innings against Lancashire, which saved his side from what looked like certain defeat, and he is also a wicket-keeper of the greatest promise.' (MacLaren.) Educated Eton. Exceptionally tall for a stumper.

C. H. TITCHMARSH (41): 'The little Titchmarsh, who was faithful to Herts when he could have done anything' (Max Reese): almost deserves a book to himself. Charles Harold Titchmarsh (known to his friends as 'Titch') had been scoring prolifically for Hertfordshire and lesser teams since the beginning of the century, refusing all offers from first-class counties to join them. Best season in 1913 (72 – 8 – 4, 106 – 147 – 62.75), including twenty five innings for Harpenden, seventeen for Herts, seven for Herts Club and Ground, seven for Cross Arrows, and three for Old Stortfordians. 56 and 26 for Gents v Players at the Oval in 1921. 'Those who do not know him must visualise a Hardstaff or a youthful Bobby Abel to obtain some idea of his stature.' (*Sporting Life.*) 'Although short of stature, he possessed a neat style of batting and strong defence, having, moreover, most of the scoring strokes at his command.' (*Herts and Cambs Reporter.*)

Capt A.C. WILKINSON (29): Alex Wilkinson was a pretty tough character who had been around. Son of a Sydney physician. Oxford Blue in 1913, but not selected in 1914. Served with distinction in the Great War, losing part of a hand. After the war, played regularly for the Army, the MCC, and the Free Foresters. Fourth in the first-class batting averages in 1922, including centuries against both universities. 'Without question one of the best Army bats of today, and there are plenty of good players in the Army who would be playing for their county could they find the time.' (MacLaren.) An opening batsman who relished taking the initiative. Unlike Fowler, no problems about getting leave for the tour: 'As I was a serving officer in the Coldstream Guards certain formalities had to be complied with, but as I was at the time serving on the staff of Major-General Sir George Jeffreys at London District all was plain sailing. I knew the General well for I had served in his brigade in France.'

G. WILSON (27): Geoffrey Wilson's career had peaked in 1913 with a memorable 173 for Harrow against Eton, taking two and a half hours for his first 50, but then scoring the rest in well faster than even time. Served in the Royal Marine Artillery. In 1919 he won a Cambridge Blue and made his debut for Yorkshire, where his family was in business. Captained Yorkshire to the county championship in 1922, though missed the last few weeks of the season through going down with appendicitis after the first day of the Roses match at Old Trafford. 'While falling short of expectation as a batsman, Mr Wilson worked very zealously.' (*Wisden.*) Short, thickset, of a quiet disposition.

Two professionals joined these eleven amateurs. Both were leg-break bowlers, chosen by MacLaren in the hope that they would be as effective on Australian wickets as Len Braund had been under his captaincy in 1901-2:

A. P. FREEMAN (35): 'Tich' Freeman was just coming into his own by this time and was at least as unlucky as Chapman not to get taken to South Africa. In the 1922 season he had taken 194 wickets for Kent, including 29 in the final week. 'Freeman was at the top of his form, keeping a remarkable length to his leg-breaks, and every now and then bowling genuine and well-disguised googlies.' (*Wisden.*) Was still hitching his trousers up as he walked back to signal his googly to the wicket-keeper.

H. TYLDESLEY (29): Harry Tyldesley was one of four cricketing sons of a Westhoughton club professional. The others were William, a batsman, who had died in the war; James, an all-rounder, who had played fairly regularly for Lancashire since 1910; and Richard, the Lancashire and England slow bowler. These Tyldesleys were not related to the brothers J. T. and Ernest. Harry had been on the ground staff at Old Trafford since before the war, making occasional appearances for the county. Like Richard, tended to roll it rather than spin it, and kept a fairly steady length. MacLaren seems to have believed in him, though can hardly have imagined that he had a second Barnes up his sleeve.

In addition to the standard expenses, Freeman and Tyldesley seem to have received a lump sum of £420 between them for making the tour, which at roughly seven pounds ten shillings per head per week (though Tyldesley probably received less than Freeman) was adequate rather than munificent. The manager of the touring party was H. D. Swan, who, in addition to his administrative work on behalf of Essex and the NZCC, was also a member of the MCC committee and, in his business life, was connected with a shipbuilding firm near Colchester. Never any great shakes as a cricketer himself, 'Swanny' from early years had enjoyed organising clubs, tours, cricket weeks and so on. He also enjoyed the sound of his own voice, but seems to have been a popular figure, if not the last word in efficiency. Honorary medical adviser on the tour was Dr Roly Pope (58), an Australian who had played for his country in 1884-85 and had subsequently accompanied most Australian teams on their tours to England. An old friend of MacLaren's, 'The Doc' had always been rich enough never to need to practise; while as a dapper little man with a passion for cricket, he had tended over the years to be an object of some fun to the cricketers themselves. Finally, four wives travelled with the team on their outward journey: the subsidised Maud MacLaren, an Australian who had the reputation for keeping Archie in check and on this tour tended to be a little cold towards the younger players, though she herself had the unfortunate habit of sometimes wearing her evening dress the wrong way round; Gladys Swan, herself a little overbearing, at least according to one survivor's memory; Muriel Wilkinson; and Dorothy Calthorpe, for whom the trip was in the nature of a honeymoon.

Physically it was a motley team indeed: most of the players were either distinctly tall (Calthorpe, Gibson, Chapman, Wilkinson, Maclean) or distinctly short (Titchmarsh, Wilson, Hill-Wood, Freeman, Tyldesley). Also, of more significance, was the striking fact that less than half of the team had been engaged in regular county cricket during the previous season. There were various other shortfalls in the composition: another left-handed batsman to join Chapman would have been an advantage; there was no bowler of genuine pace; and a slow left-armer was also lacking. Nevertheless, for all that, it was still a team which contained an attractive (even eccentric) mixture of experienced and promising players, though one or two arguably fell in neither category. Press reaction in both Australia and New Zealand when the team was announced was that it was a party of 'picnic tourists', but that manifestly was an exaggeration. MacLaren himself, on the eve of departure, weighed up his team's prospects on and off the field:

I cannot help feeling that the bowling is our greatest strength and that we may get teams out more cheaply than expected, and that our batting may not overcome the bowling of the Australians in the same way as our bowlers may beat our opponents' batting. In New Zealand the cricket is not considered to be of quite the same high standard as in Australia, in spite of there being many good cricketers in the country, and it remains to be seen of what we are capable against them, the only certainty being that we will enjoy the cricket to the full, and be treated right royally wherever we play.

* * * * * *

'Swanny'

Saturday morning, September 30, was departure date: 'As the
9.15 train pulled out from St Pancras today, a pretty girl dashed
forward and flung a bunch of white heather into a saloon
compartment. It was her "good luck" offering to the MCC
team . . . .' And the *Evening News* reporter added: 'Hill-Wood's
expressive grin was the last impression the party on the platform
had as the train steamed out. His luggage was a joy to behold –
striped gorgeously in yellow and red and blue, to aid him in
picking it out.' Among those seeing the party off was Johnny
Douglas, who, asked about MacLaren, said 'We may see some
glimpses of his old form when he gets into the sunshine'.
Maclaren, however, was not one of those who later in the
morning embarked at Tilbury on the S.S. *Orvieto*: along with
his wife, the Swans, the Wilkinsons, Hartley, and Gibson, he
preferred to catch a train to Toulon the following Thursday and
embark there. The main event of the voyage was a one-day
game in Colombo that a Ceylonese, F. L. Gunawardene, travelling on the ship, had persuaded MacLaren to play. Wilson (still
recovering from his operation), Freeman, and MacLaren himself stood down, as on a day of stupefying mugginess Ceylon
reached 147 for 5 declared. A crowd of some 10,000 was duly
impressed by Chapman's fielding at cover, though Chapman
himself had afterwards to wring the sweat out of his trousers.
MCC in reply were 100 for 4, in very bad light, when rain
stopped play. Titchmarsh top scored with 41: 'The perspiration
was pouring off him, and he called for a towel. One was brought
from the Pavilion and, after he had wiped his face, the umpire
offered to take care of it. Titchmarsh, however, would have
none of it, waving him away and stuffing the towel into his
trouser pocket, in order to make sure of its being handy.
Then after every run, he threw his bat on the ground and gazed
at it with a "more in sorrow than in anger" sort of expression,
while between overs he laid down as though in a state of utter
exhaustion.' There followed in the evening a big dinner, at
which so much was drunk that Wilson fell out of the launch on
the way back to the *Orvieto*. But he was retrieved and the ship set
forth for Australia, leaving MacLaren merely to send the ritual
parting telegram to the Ceylon Cricket Association: 'The boys
delighted with their day and their great welcome'.

The team reached Perth on the morning of November 2 and were met there by W. H. Ferguson, who had come across from Sydney to act as scorer and baggage man for the rest of the tour, an even more inevitable presence than that of Roly Pope. Ferguson himself later recalled how 'at the very start of the tour, Mr MacLaren told me, "Fergie, this Mr Swan is a very nice chap, but as a manager he's hopeless, so you'd better take charge of everything"'. MacLaren gave various interviews to the local press, declaring that his job of captaincy 'was a pleasure, because they were a fine lot of boys and he was charmed with the task of bringing to the surface their undoubted talents'. But 'with regard to himself, he feared he had long since passed the day of long scores made by good batting'. The interviews over, MacLaren then returned to the *Orvieto* and, in the company of Calthorpe, Wilson, and Maclean, sailed straight on to Adelaide, leaving the others to play the two-day match against Western Australia without the benefit of his tutelage. According to Wilkinson, he was 'looking forward so much to seeing his old friend, Clem Hill, in Adelaide', even hoping that he might persuade him to play one last time against the English.

Meanwhile, back in Perth, Swan was forced to turn out and, batting at number eleven, was bowled by Bott for a duck as MCC struggled to 190 only a day after they had landed. 'The Englishmen were greatly troubled by the humid heat and frequent dust squalls,' Reuter reported. Chapman made 75 with 'some beautiful shots all round the wicket', Wilkinson a solid 40, and Lowry a brisk 20 ('forceful from the jump'), but the last seven wickets added only 43 runs. Western Australia replied with 234, Gibson and Freeman bowling 38 eight-ball overs each and Lowry keeping wicket, and MCC were 132 for 3 when the match ended. In that second innings, Titchmarsh found his antipodean feet with a steady 50 not out, mostly cuts and pulls, while Chapman's 58 in thirty nine minutes 'was a sparkling display which pleased immensely', according to the *West Australian*. The team then viewed a few trotting races, but by the end of the evening were on the Trans-train for Adelaide, an arduous journey taking three days and, because of different gauges, involving five changes of train. 'Still, as several of us were interested in the Royal and Ancient game of Bridge',

Wilkinson later recalled, 'we kept ourselves amused.'

They arrived to find MacLaren well ensconced, giving interviews and trying unsuccessfully to have six-ball overs in the coming match with South Australia. On the first morning 'MacLaren was warmly applauded as he led his team into the field', but that was where his pleasure must have ended as A. J. and V. Y. Richardson (unrelated) put on 256 for the first wicket in 125 minutes and South Australia (without Hill) totalled 442. The local *Advertiser* reported that Tyldesley, 5 for 100, 'bowled well throughout'; that with Maclean still ill, Lowry and Titchmarsh shared duties behind the stumps; and that 'Chapman is a wonder in the field, nothing finer than his picking up and

Wilkinson and Chapman batting at Adelaide

returning having been seen on this oval for years'. Indeed, so stunning was Chapman's display on this first day at Adelaide that, according to another account, 'critics with long memories say he compared favourably with Vernon Royle, the master who came to Australia in 1878-79 with Lord Harris's team'. Interestingly, MacLaren a couple of years later recalled that throughout the tour he had instructed his bowlers to feed extra cover, for there in Chapman lay the side's strength in fielding. Highlight of the Saturday, as MCC batted rather stodgily to make 205 and 38 for 1, came after the fall of the fifth wicket: 'The

Practise at Sydney: Maclean, Tyldesley, Wilkinson

41

appearance of MacLaren was marked by loud and continuous applause, followed by the South Australian team doffing their headgear and giving the veteran three ringing cheers. A roar of approval from the crowd [some 7,500] signalised the English captain's first stroke, which was a beautiful hit to the leg boundary.' There followed some more nostalgia-laden strokes before he was caught and bowled for 12, having already been dropped at mid-on off a full toss. Monday saw a dramatic finish. MCC totalled 294 (Wilson 61 in 150 minutes, MacLaren 41 in ninety seven minutes), leaving South Australia twenty two minutes to make 58. Whereupon 'MacLaren showed true sporting spirit by taking the field again promptly and by putting on two slow bowlers – Freeman and Tyldesley.' Naturally he 'dotted the fieldsmen round the boundary line', but South Australia got home by six wickets with a minute or so to spare, Freeman in the process taking a chaotic sort of hat trick. That at least was some of the 'sporting cricket' MacLaren had promised before the tour.

The following day the team travelled by express to Melbourne, where, according to Ferguson, 'MacLaren decided he did not like the hotel allotted to the team, so he sought out the best hotel in town and moved over'. The first day against Victoria featured another round of sustained cheering for the veteran, but 'just a reminiscence of that typical late chopping cut in the slips' was all he could show before being caught behind for 5. MCC made only 210 (Chapman stumped for 73 running out to a Hartkopf donkey drop), but it did not seem such a bad score when Victoria were 44 for 5 at stumps. Three of those wickets fell to Gibson, prompting a detailed description of his bowling style in the *Argus*: 'Coming up with a quick run and nice easy action, his arm and the ball at the last moment completely disappear behind him, and in the delivery the ball comes from the middle of his back.' One wicket that evaded him was Liddicut's: 'The Victorians had been batting so feebly against the slows . . . that a silly-point was utilised. Freeman sent one down to Woodfull, who stepped out and drove it hard against Gibson's leg, who was fielding close in; the ball ricocheted towards the bowler, who made a grab at it but failed to hold it, whence it cannoned on to the wicket . . . . As Liddicut was standing outside his

crease, seemingly unable to grasp the situation, he was run out.'
Victoria later recovered to 278, MCC made 231 (Titchmarsh
82, MacLaren 0), and Victoria, thanks to some dropped catches,
squeezed through by two wickets, Calthorpe 4 for 41. 'The
honours of the game were mainly with the losing side', the *Argus*
stated, though the *Australasian*'s correspondent criticised
Freeman and Tyldesley for not spinning the ball enough and
quoted one of the MCC team: 'My word, I wish we had a
bowler that could turn the ball like Hartkopf'. An interested
spectator was Marcus Marks, New Zealand's former Government Printer, who sent a pithy report to a paper in Wellington:
'Saw MacLaren's team play; they are too good for New Zealand,
but will be pleasant to see. MacLaren is done, but young
Chapman is splendid – a great bat and the finest fielder I have
seen.' Ferguson, however, has the last word on the Melbourne
leg: 'On the day we left, I was unlucky enough to be stationed in
the hall when Mr MacLaren was paying the bill, and he called
to me, "Lend me some cash. I haven't got enough to settle the
champagne account".'

On to Sydney where, to judge by Wilkinson's account,
arrangements ran true to form: 'There was one thing Archie
liked and that was comfort. So when we found ourselves parked
in a more or less glorified hut, we were moved out to Australia
Hotel at Archie's behest.' The match against New South Wales
was the tourists' sternest test, with the state team including
seven of the Australian tourists of 1921, but all the honours
on the first day went to the MCC, for whom three batsmen
dominated in a total of 360: Chapman with a century in 78
minutes that Ferguson at the time reckoned the finest innings
he had even seen; Titchmarsh, 'a paragon of care and patience',
with 79; and MacLaren, whose 54, 'played with all his old-time
grace', was scored after intensely emotional scenes greeted his
return to the arena of some of his greatest triumphs. Saturday
was no less remarkable a day, as first the improbable duo
of Brand and Tyldesley ('stout and seemingly cumbersome')
skittled out New South Wales for 201, inspiring another ovation
for MacLaren as he led his team back into the pavilion; and
then MCC themselves, MacLaren not enforcing the follow-on,
got into trouble to reach 117 for 9 at close of play, MacLaren 26

not out. Even more convinced than he had been earlier in the afternoon that the wicket would not last, MacLaren then went into the dressing-room and, again according to Wilkinson, threw his bat on the table saying, 'No one could make 150 on that wicket against our bowling'. But Wilkinson's account continues: 'There was a very local shower on the Sydney Cricket Ground on the Sunday . . . . When Archie went in on Monday his partner [Tyldesley] was quickly dismissed, leaving Archie 28 not out. When he got into the dressing-room he exploded! The wicket had been watered. As a result, New South Wales had a perfect wicket to bat on and knocked off their 280 runs for the loss of five wickets.' Macartney scored a masterly 84, Gibson took three wickets, and first slip was left to rue his luck.

* * * * * *

Preparations in New Zealand continued apace. In October, following correspondence in London between Bell and the MCC, the NZCC confirmed Bell's action 'in agreeing to allow the cost of washing as an expense together with all necessary tips, paid out by the manager for the team instead of each individual member being allowed this privilege'. At the end of November the NZCC considered a request from across the Tasman:

Mr H. D. Swan, in a letter to the chairman, expressed the wish of himself and Mr MacLaren that the team should be accommodated at the best hotels, specially mentioning the Grand Hotel, Auckland, and Midland Hotel, Wellington. The committee had previously accepted the terms offered by the Star Hotel, Auckland, and Grand Hotel, Wellington. Whilst the change as desired by the manager of the team would mean an additional expense of £124, in the course of a lengthy discussion various reasons were put forward as to why the wishes of Messrs Swan and MacLaren should be acceded to if at all possible.

Reluctantly, by five votes to two, their wishes were acceded to. A happier task for the NZCC was to agree that, for the first time in New Zealand's cricket history, all the matches against the English tourists would be played by teams of eleven men. 'It is quite apart from the principle of cricket, as it should be played, to have one side numerically stronger than the other', declared the chairman of the management committee, J. S. Barrett. However, some internal friction prevailed when it came to deciding how the national team would be chosen for the three 'Tests' that lay ahead. The old Wellington player, Ken Tucker, had been sole selector for the Australian tour of 1920-21, but now it was decided that he should be joined by Nesbit Snedden of Auckland and Alex Martin of Dunedin. Snedden, a solicitor in real life, was a fair enough choice, being Auckland's current captain and the likely captain of the New Zealand team; but Martin, a tailor, was a different matter, since he seems to have known relatively little about cricket and was guided in his approach to the game more by social than by playing considerations. Anyway, for whatever reasons, Tucker took umbrage, and it was only by dint of persevering negotiations that he was persuaded to withdraw his resignation. Selection by remote triumvirate it would be.

A possible rival to Snedden as captain was Wellington's powerfully-built Stan 'Sixer' Brice, who (along with Snedden) had been one of New Zealand's captains in the 1920-21 series. Brice had had a strange career. Before the war he had been a tear-away fast bowler playing in the shadow of the similar but more accurate style of Ernest Upham, with the result that in twelve seasons he had taken only 46 first-class wickets (though of course no New Zealand player at this stage ever played more than a handful of first-class matches in a season). Now, however, in his early forties, Brice had emerged as perhaps the best bowler in New Zealand, at a little above medium and making the ball swerve as well as break back. He also had an outswinger and was particularly skilful at using the invariable wind swirling round the Basin Reserve at Wellington. As a captain he is described by Arthur Carman as 'a fine and wily tactician'; while as an immensely popular character, the Wellington *Evening Post*'s description of him as 'a good sport, quiet and unassuming', hit the mark. He worked as chief engineer at the Great Meat Company in Petone, Wellington. As a batsman he was renowned for his big hitting, but by 1922, as one paper put it, 'of recent years he has not troubled the scorers overmuch'. The new club season in Wellington began slowly, with rain stopping all play on successive Saturdays, but on November 25 Brice was into his stride with a vengeance, scoring 228 in 205 minutes for Petone against YMCA at the Petone Recreation Ground. 'Brice's play was full of vim, and eight times he sent the leather soaring over the boundary line for six.' The following Saturday he was equally vim-full, taking 6 for 10 as YMCA collapsed for 31, sending the youngsters firmly to the foot of the local league table. Brice had, as they say, put down a marker.

Meanwhile, as committees considered and Brice biffed, there began to flit across the face of New Zealand cricket the shadowy figure of B. J. Kortlang. Old Wellingtonians remembered him in later years with respect rather than affection: 'A typical Australian, hard-hitter, laconic, imperturbable ... a heavy scorer, full of confidence and a most difficult batsman to dismiss ... a fearless close fielder in front of the bat . . . a hard shot'. Such was Carman's verdict, to be tempered by that of another cricketer of the twenties: 'A typical Australian . . . a real bloody show-off ... a wise-guy type'. In 1922, however, little was generally known about Bert Kortlang as a cricketer, apart from the fact that he had been a successful opening batsman for Victoria for a season or two before the war, and still less was known about his life off the field, apart from the fact that he had travelled widely. 'Touchline' of the *New Zealand Free Lance* reported at the beginning of November that he had recently seen Kortlang in Wellington: 'Although his movements are a bit uncertain, he told me that he hopes to get a season's cricket here. He will be in and out of Wellington during this month, and maybe by the beginning of December he may so arrange things as to be able to settle down here for a few months.' While soon afterwards the Wellington correspondent of the *Weekly Press* noted that, in a chat with him, Kortlang had declared that 'he had got tired of his junkettings about' and was looking to settle for a bit. And indeed, by early in December he was back in Wellington, ready to play to the full his part as joker in the new season's pack.

* * * * * *

MacLaren and his men had a hard time actually getting across the Tasman. Even before the match with New South Wales ended on November 27, a shipping strike affecting both Australia and New Zealand had the NZCC (responsible for all travel arrangements) acting quickly, as Barrett told the press on the 22nd: 'The Council had decided to avoid any possible derangement by "pencilling" berths on the *Ulimaroa*, which was scheduled to leave Sydney before the *Makura*, by which vessel it had been intended that MacLaren's team should travel. The only difference would be that the team would disembark in Wellington, and proceed north immediately for their match with Auckland.' On December 1 MacLaren celebrated his 51st birthday; and on the 2nd the team boarded the *Ulimaroa*, only to find that not only did the crew refuse to sail until six dismissed firemen had been reinstated, but also that the 'immobilised' *Makura* was in fact calmly leaving Sydney bound for Auckland. There then followed a heels-kicking week in Sydney, causing the no doubt penitent NZCC to rearrange the whole schedule of the tour, including putting back the opening match in Auckland from the 8th to the 15th. Finally, however, on the 8th, the team did get away, leaving Sydney for Auckland on the *Moeraki*, mostly manned by British blacklegs. Mid-way across the stokers went on strike, the ship lay becalmed for some hours, and several of the team went down to do some stoking themselves, Chapman to the fore. They eventually made landfall on the afternoon of Wednesday the 13th. Yet again missing all the fun was MacLaren, who at the last moment had switched to the *Ulimaroa*, on which his wife (a poor sailor) was booked and which left Sydney on the 9th for Wellington. There, 'looking a good deal older, and fuller round the waist-line, but none the less alert and keen', he arrived on the morning of the 13th, just too late to catch the mid-day express for Auckland.

A Popular Cricketer and his Wife: Mr and Mrs A.C. MacLaren

·3·

MacLaren deplores commercialism — accommodation problems in Auckland — lost ball in Wanganui — Chapman captures Dominion's heart — MacLaren gets the shakes — Kortlang on song — a nation expects

Resigned to spending the night in Wellington, MacLaren installed himself in the Midland Hotel and proceeded to give a wide-ranging press conference. About himself: 'My sight is still good, but I cannot time them as of yore, and the ball hurts when it hits me much more than it did twenty years ago.' And he added that he had given up smoking for the duration of the tour, not wanting to appear as 'a lumbering cart horse among a lot of colts'. About his team's prospects: 'I am quite in the dark as to New Zealand cricket, but I think you will find that we shall give you a good game . . . . You will probably find that this side will not take a lot of getting out, but bowling is our strength, and we shall be more difficult to get runs against . . . . When I see the strength of your side I may prefer to leave the professionals out of our side, and so make it purely amateur, but that all depends on how you shape against us. If you commence to hit us about, then we will have to keep our professionals.' On being told that he would have to decide which was the best ground his team had played on, for the purpose of awarding a prize to the winning groundsman: 'That's a nice thing to put on to me'. And about the underlying spirit of the whole venture: 'Touring abroad improves the young player's cricket. It gives the young player a greater amount of experience of grounds, foreign crowds, and it gives him the confidence which leads to success. It gives him an opportunity of playing cricket which is rather different to that which is played at Home. County cricket has got that commercial ring about it, but out here it is sporting cricket all the way through, with a team like this.' All that said, MacLaren then called in briefly for a first look at the Basin Reserve before going on to Wellington College, where the school was playing C. G. Wilson's Eleven. Batting at number four for Wilson's team was Kortlang, who scored 18 and sustained a knock in the process. 'At the conclusion of Wellington College's innings, Mr MacLaren was introduced to each of the boys, and expressed himself as well satisfied with the standard of play they had shown.' The following morning he caught the train to Auckland, reaching there on the Friday morning only a few hours before the start of play.

In Auckland itself, the arrival there of the rest of the team had not been without its problematic undertones. The amateurs moved into the Grand Hotel, while the professionals were accommodated elsewhere, probably at the rejected Star. Ferguson tells the story: 'I asked Mr Swan what hotel he proposed I should stay at, and he answered, "You must live at the same place as the professionals". Resenting the class distinction, I made it very clear that I considered myself well enough behaved to stay with the main party at the Grand Hotel, and he agreed, saying, "We shall be pleased to allow you to stay with us".' Whereupon Ferguson then announced that he would prefer to stay with the professionals, though not before 'Mr Swan actually told me that Freeman and Tyldesley had been brought to Auckland as servants of the team'. Centre-piece of the following day, Thursday, was a full-scale civic reception, where the *Auckland Star* was forcibly struck by 'the boyishness of the team'. The Mayor's speech duly set the standard for the many mayoral addresses that stretched ahead:

Cricket, he said, was pre-eminently the game of all the games that entered so largely into British national life, and although we were as yet a young country, he hoped the visitors would find that we were a people of the true British stock . . . . After incidental reference to the

T. C. Lowry | A. P. F. Chapman | Lieut.-Colonel J. C. Hartley | Hon. D. F. Brand

C. H. Gibson | A. C. Wilkinson | C. H. Titchmarsh | G. Wilson

V. W. Hill-Wood | A. P. Freeman | Hon. F. S. G. Calthorpe | J. F. Maclean

51

part played by New Zealand in imperial football, tennis, athletics, and aquatics, and the wonderful place taken by Australia in international cricket, without missing the moral that the bonds of Empire had been strengthened largely by sport, Mr Gunson paid a tribute to the generous assistance given New Zealand in her slower development of cricket by Australia and by the MCC . . . . What he particularly desired was that the players should catch the spirit of New Zealand, as it was seen by the late Lord Northcliffe, who stated after his visit here last year that he had found New Zealand the most British of all the lands outside Britain he had visited . . . . Mr Gunson concluded by assuring the team it would have a thoroughly hearty welcome in all parts of the country, and by wishing them "Kia Ora".

Colonel Hartley in reply promised that the team would play 'a sporting and entertaining game', though he also 'mentioned the great difficulties experienced in these post-war days in England, when everybody had to work more and had not the leisure of the old days, in getting a team for such a tour as this'. Final preliminary formalities were completed on Friday morning. While MacLaren snatched a few hours' rest in the hotel, it was agreed that all the matches on the tour would be played with six-ball overs, as stipulated by the MCC, even though New Zealand's domestic cricket was at the time unofficially following the Australian eight-ball example. The longer over had its snags, for at Dunedin later in the season the experiment was tried, successfully it seems, of sounding a gong at the end of each over in order to tell the umpires that the eighth ball had been delivered.

Man for man, Auckland had at this time probably the best side in New Zealand. 'Nessie' Snedden, apart from being 'a good leader with a sound knowledge of the game' (T. W. Reese), was also a reliable batsman and useful medium-pace bowler who in his youth had benefited much from Relf's coaching. Other all-rounders in the team included Raoul Garrard, a tall accountant who bowled leg-breaks, and Cyril Allcott, a bank officer who bowled accurate slow to medium left-arm orthodox. Allcott came from Nelson (for whom as a seventeen year old he had played against Trumper *et al* in 1914), then went to Blenheim, and only moved to Auckland on the urging of friends that he had no future as a cricketer unless he was living in one of the main cities. Wicket-keeper was Dick Rowntree, who as a young man had played for Yorkshire Second Eleven, had been compelled through illness to emigrate in 1905, and was now, in his late thirties, indisputably the best in New Zealand. An emerging batsman in the team was the left-handed Eddie McLeod, a design engineer in the railways who had hit his first ball in provincial cricket for a straight six. A much better-known figure, though, was Ces Dacre, the dashing batsman and brilliant fielder who on Boxing Day 1914, aged fifteen years and seven months, had made his first-class debut for Auckland against Wellington, wearing long trousers for the first time in his life. Since the war he had been a regular in the Auckland team and had played twice against Australia in 1920-21. Like Chapman he had a very fast left-hand throw that was almost under-arm and, like Chapman, his promise was immense.

There was no more interesting cricketer in the Auckland side, however, than S.G. Smith, the man of three careers. Sidney Smith was born at San Fernando, Trinidad in 1881 into a plantation-owning family and by the turn of the century was shining for Trinidad as a left-handed all-rounder. In 1901-2, for All West Indies against R.A. Bennett's team of English amateurs (including Bosanquet), his slows achieved match figures of 16 for 85. In 1906 he toured England with H.B.G. Austin's West Indian team and in all matches topped both the batting and bowling averages, turning in such a fine performance against Northamptonshire that that county offered him the assistant secretaryship and he began qualifying the following season. For the last six seasons before the war he was a mainstay of the Northants side, which in 1912 very nearly won the champion-ship. In 1913 he was appointed county captain; on several occasions he represented the Gentlemen; and in 1915 he was one of *Wisden*'s Five Cricketers of the Year: 'A very individual cricketer . . . a dangerous bat on slow wickets . . . his bowling offers endless temptations to batsmen, but thanks to the certainty of his pitch he is by no means easy to hit'. Then in 1915, on account of his wife's asthma, he emigrated to Auckland, taking up a position as an insurance accountant. After the war he was an automatic choice for the province, scoring 256 against Canterbury in 1919-20. He seems to have been a pretty assertive character, not short of verbals on the pitch, but with a sardonic sense of humour. His style was distinctive: he always bowled with his sleeves down and had the mesmerising habit of shaking his left hand at the top of his action before, with an apparently bent arm, he jerked the ball out almost like throwing a dart. 'Not so dangerous a bowler as when he first settled in Auckland' was the view of one paper, but according to the *New Zealand Herald*, 'Smith is essentially a "big" cricket man, and against the English eleven may be expected to do well.'

In the event, it was the medium-slow Arnold Anthony who took the bowling honours for Auckland, with 6 for 43 as MCC totalled 350. Titchmarsh made an almost chanceless 154, but inevitably the main focus was on MacLaren, who opened the batting for the first time on the tour and scored 58, including ten boundaries: 'One can imagine how the bowling would have suffered had he had his former quickness of foot in dealing with leg shots, to give them the spanking character which characterised his cover drives.' At one point on the Friday, as the rain which had delayed the start was still falling, MacLaren asked Snedden if he would like to leave the field, but he declined, saying that Auckland was used to such conditions. More rain fell the following day, blotting out the morning session, whereupon the MCC innings was completed (Smith picking up his only two wickets, Brand and Gibson) and Auckland reached 107 for 5 by close of play. It was not easy going:

A shower of rain caused an adjournment of twenty minutes, and made the wicket slushy. After playing an over on the treacherous foothold, Snedden held a consultation with MacLaren and the umpires about the state of the pitch, and they left the decision to him. There was, however, such a clamour from the crowd [a biggish Saturday one] when they saw what was afoot that Snedden played on against his better judgement, and at once MacLaren, like a good tactician, whipped on his slow bowlers, so that to get runs the batsmen had to move about the slippery wicket.

In the absence of the two leg-breaking serfs, these slow bowlers were Brand (4 for 31, cutting down his pace) and Hill-Wood (0 for 35, tossing them up very high). Snedden made 18, before,

The MCC team photographed with the Governor-General at Eden Park:
Sitting: *H. D. Swan (hon. team manager), A. C. MacLaren (captain),*
Viscount Jellicoe, Lieut-Colonel J. C. Hartley (vice-captain), T. C. Lowry,
C. H. Gibson
Standing: *J. F. Maclean, A. P. Freeman, A. P. F. Chapman,*
A. C. Wilkinson, G. Wilson, C. H. Titchmarsh, H. Tyldesley,
W. W. Hill-Wood, W. Ferguson (scorer), Hon D. F. Brand,
Hon F. S. G. Calthorpe

slipping on the wet wicket, he gave a catch to Chapman.
Otherwise, Smith scored 25 and Garrard 37 not out, making full
use of his 'fine reach and loose-limbed action'.

The main events of the weekend took place off the field.
Jellicoe did his stuff by giving a lavish party for the team and
also inviting the MacLarens, the Wilkinsons, and Brand to be
his guests at Government House. MacLaren found himself
particularly busy answering journalists' questions in the wake
of the English response to the remarks he had himself uttered
in Wellington about the 'commercial ring' of county cricket.
Typical of the response was Lionel Tennyson's reported comment: 'The game is no more commercialised here than in

Australia. Professionalism is the backbone of English county cricket. I cannot understand what Mr MacLaren is driving at; force of habit is the possible explanation.' Put on the defensive, MacLaren now contented himself with pointing out how poorly England's professionals had fared in the previous ten Tests against Australia and drawing attention to the deeds of Brand and Gibson in the recent match in Sydney. The final two days in Auckland were characterised by a mild sense of bathos: on Sunday an ill-advised launch trip led to MacLaren complaining of neuralgia; and on Monday rain washed out all play. That evening the tourists caught the 7.10 train for Wanganui, changing at Marton and arriving at 11.17 a.m.

Elsewhere in New Zealand, the season's cricket was still entirely confined to local grade level, but on Saturday the 16th, despite his mid-week injury, Kortlang did make his debut for Wellington (the club) versus YMCA at Basin Reserve No. 1. YMCA scored 276, with 'Father' Wilson (by now retired as a first-class cricketer) taking 5 for 17 in a devastating spell late in the innings. Wellington at stumps were 117 for 2: Bernau was 49 not out and Kortlang 44 not out, 'shaping in good style'. On the Monday, as it rained in Auckland, the NZCC met in Christchurch to consider some of the small change of hosting a tour: 'The committee confirmed the secretary's action in reference to telegram from Auckland Association advising that they had been approached by the manager of the English team to pay tips amounting to fifteen pounds.' And: 'Mrs MacLaren's railway fare from Wellington to Auckland. The Minister of Railways wired if this was to be charged to the Council. The secretary's action was approved of in replying that the Council was to stand this expense.'

On Tuesday and Wednesday the tourists played a two-day match at Wanganui against a combined team representing the North and South Taranaki, Wanganui, and Waikato Associations. Apart from the civic reception, where MacLaren was assured that 'there was no commercialism in the game in New Zealand and that they played the game here for the love of it', there were various other pleasures at hand: on Tuesday evening both teams were entertained at His Majesty's Theatre and enjoyed a triple bill on the big screen of *The Prodigal Judge*, *The*

Barnyard Cavalier (a burlesque of the Three Musketeers), and *Disraeli*, starring George Arliss in the film version of Louis N. Parker's play of that name; while on Wednesday evening the visitors were given a choice between a drive to Castlecliff (the local beach) or a boat excursion up the much more beautiful Wanganui River. Mrs MacLaren was certainly around during these two days, to judge by a story told soon afterwards by Barrett of the NZCC to a reporter: 'The Minor Associations looked like making a stand, and Mrs MacLaren, taking advantage of a chance to communicate with her husband, by sending him a pencilled note, suggested a change in the bowling. The sham indignation of the veteran was most amusing. "For twenty five years", he said, "my wife has bossed me in the house, but I'll be *** if she will do it on the cricket field". Strangely enough, the suggested change in the bowling was made, and duly came off.' Battling away against these insuperable odds, the combined team included two players of particular interest. One was the Rev E. O. Blamires, known as 'The Cricketing Cleric' and described by Carman as 'a tall, solid-scoring batsman and teasing slow bowler', though on this occasion he had to keep wicket. Blamires, a Methodist, was an Australian who had come to New Zealand in 1903 and whose ministry had taken him before the war to Otago and Wellington (representing both in the Plunket Shield) and now to Wairarapa. From a younger generation was North Taranaki's Herb Lambert, a hard-hitting batsman and medium-pace bowler who had enjoyed some successful seasons for Wellington immediately after the war. According to the *Wanganui Herald*, he 'first rose to fame locally at a dinner function by asking for the "witticks" to be passed, said "witticks" being asparagus'.

The match itself at Cook's Gardens, starting at two o'clock on a bitterly cold day in front of a meagre crowd that gradually grew, was a one-sided affair. Lambert batted boldly for 66 in fifty two minutes, but Blamires was bowled by Gibson for 5 and the combined team could muster only 129. Pick of the bowlers was Brand (3 for 30), who 'mixed his pace cleverly and bowled a fast yorker with little change of action'. Calthorpe, dropped in the slips on 0 and 4, then scored an aggressive 117, as MCC batted on into Wednesday to reach 296 and the combined team lost their fast bowler, C. A. Holland, to injury after he had bowled only seven overs. Major disappointment of the innings was Chapman, who 'seemed nonplussed by the pace of the wicket, and after cocking a couple of balls up and fluking a single he was clean bowled'. MacLaren, batting down the order again, on drove and cover drove Waikato's Gilmour for four apiece, but 'played forward at the next, a beautiful length ball which skimmed his bails off', dismissing him for 12. In his unaccustomed role behind the wicket, Blamires 'stood right up to the stumps and did well'. The combined team improved second time round, totalling 200, with Lambert 63 and Blamires 31. Gibson took 5 for 72, but the *Wanganui Chronicle* reserved its main praise for the fielding: 'Chapman was energy personified as cover, and his lightning return was a theme for admiration. Wilkinson was in the limelight for clean work and a glorious one-handed catch at square leg which occasioned Blamires' downfall. But all the team can field, and even the portly Mac-Laren showed an alertness that was surprising.' Lowry and Hill-Wood then quickly knocked off the required 34 runs, after which: 'A few extra overs were played, the game being brought to a conclusion as the result of a sensational hit by Lowry, who sent the ball flying over the stand into the backyard of one of the Wilson Street residences. Though a crowd searched, the ball was not forthcoming, and play thus ended.'

While the tourists then travelled south – on Thursday to Wellington, where they caught the overnight ferry to Lyttleton – the New Zealand selectors announced the team for the First 'Test', due to start at Wellington on Saturday the 30th. It showed a strong bias towards North Island: Snedden, Smith, McLeod, Garrard, Allcott, and Rowntree (Auckland); Hiddleston, Collins, and Brice (Wellington); Blunt (Canterbury); and Shepherd (Otago); twelfth man: Galland (Otago). The main criticism that the announcement evoked was the omission of Dacre and Lambert, while in Wellington there was a certain local rumbling about Snedden rather than Brice or Collins being given the captaincy. David Collins certainly had a fine pedigree. His father, Dr W. E. Collins, had played for Wellington in the 1880s, while he himself, while still a boy at Wellington College, had made his debut for Wellington in 1906,

At Wanganui

soon afterwards carrying his bat against Canterbury. Collins
then went to Cambridge, where he became 'the last "Double-
Blue" in the true and traditional sense of the XI and the
Boat' (Altham.) In 1910, as Cambridge collapsed to Oxford's
P. R. Le Couteur, he made 31 out of a total of 76; and the
following year, opening the batting, his scores in the Varsity
match were 57 and 50. After the war he confined his cricket to
playing for Wairarapa, where he had started farming, until
Wellington in 1921-22 persuaded him to turn out for them
again. For the new season he had agreed to take over Wellington's captaincy. Described by Don Neely as 'a fine forceful
batsman and a most competent leader of men', Collins always
batted with his sleeves buttoned down and conveyed a general
air of elegance at the crease, though at this stage of his career
he was handicapped by lack of practice. He had, perhaps
surprisingly, a superstitious streak, for he also always used to
bat in his Cambridge cap and, according to a story told by
Eddie McLeod, he once found in Dunedin that it was missing

59

The New Zealand team in the First 'Test':
Back row: *J. W. Condliffe, R. C. Blunt, D. R. Garrard, E. McLeod, C. Allcott*
Front row: *A. Galland, J. S. Shepherd, D. C. Collins, N. C. Snedden (captain), S. G. Smith, J. S. Hiddleston, W. S. Brice*

from his bag, declared that he would not get any runs, and duly collected a pair.

Collins was not New Zealand's leading batsman, for few judges at this time would have placed anyone above Sid Hiddleston, rated by the Australians in 1920-21 as the best in the country. As enjoyably assertive a character as he was a batsman, he had stayed in Wellington after the war and scored as an opener with great consistency, while also turning in some useful figures with his slow to medium breaks. 'There were several innings by Hiddleston where his dominating figure took command as soon as he arrived at the crease. His theory was that the first ball should be hit for four, so that the batsman got on top of the bowler right from the outset.' Carman's memory is shared by other contemporaries, who recall especially the power and precision of Hiddleston's cutting. While 'Curly' Page, New Zealand's captain in the 1930s, states simply of Hiddleston: 'The best of them all, bar none'.

The two Otago players featuring in the squad enjoy less retrospective lustre, but were both capable operators. Jim Shepherd had played for Otago before the war, but was now emerging as that province's leading batsman. He was, according to T. W. Reese, renowned for his 'forceful back-stroke play' and also bowled quite useful medium-pace. A shy, retiring sort of person, he worked for a firm of saddlers and was an elder of the Presbyterian Church in Dunedin. Rather more of a 'character' was Arthur ('Gal') Galland, who captained Otago and was an aggressive batsman, persevering stock bowler, and safe slip. He was a no-nonsense cricketer and a plumber by trade, with a reputation for not charging those who were too poor to pay. Also unlike most leading New Zealand players (who tended to come from the professional class) was the fact that he was a prominent rugby player, which tended to make for a distinctive type of cricketer. Tactics were not his strong point as Otago's captain, but his presence was invaluable.

For their final match before the First 'Test', the MCC team arrived at Christchurch railway station on the morning of Friday the 22nd. 'There was no mistaking the veteran leader Mr A. C. MacLaren, who was wearing white flannel trousers . . . . On the platform was F. Shacklock, once of Derby and Notts, veteran coach of the Canterbury Boys' Association. Mr MacLaren soon espied him. "Hello, Shacklock!" was his greeting, and for a few minutes the two indulged in reminiscences of old times in English county cricket.' The Christchurch *Sun* then described MacLaren's charges: 'The members of the team are mainly a tall, cleanly-built, fresh-looking lot, sporting ties with the MCC colours – red, blue, green, and yellow – a combination which certainly hits the eye.' And the verdict of Dr Roly Pope was quoted: 'They are a fine lot of boys, and I'm proud to be with them.' Arrangements in Christchurch took the form of the amateurs staying at the United Service Hotel and the professionals at the Clarendon, though on Satur-

'Bathing Party at Christchurch'
Hartley, Dorothy Calthorpe, Willie Hill-Wood

day evening Freeman and Tyldesley did attend the dance given in honour of the team by Mr and Mrs George Gould at their home, 'Avonbank', Fendalton. The civic reception on Friday included a ponderous piece of deputy-mayoral humour: 'He could not present them with the freedom of the city, but he would present them with the freedom of the city baths – not that he wished to suggest that they needed it. (Laughter)'. By far the most interesting speech was given by Dan Reese, speaking as a member of the NZCC:

He agreed that visits by English teams were infrequent. They involved the Council in a very heavy financial responsibility, and it was no easy matter for a committee, sitting at a table in New Zealand, to organise tours of the kind. He believed that Mr MacLaren's side was a re-compense for all the trouble which the Council had taken. New Zealand had always been enterprising in the matter of English tours, the first of which had taken place in 1864. Then the contest had been between Englishmen and Englishmen; now the visitors would meet the grandsons of the pioneers. New Zealand realised the greatness of the MCC, which controlled cricket throughout the world, and yet remained a private club. It was still conservative in some of its ways, and its constitution was not democratic enough to suit the ideas of cricketers overseas, but though they could not quite understand it they admired it as a great institution.

Even more indicative of local feeling at this stage of the tour was the editorial that appeared that morning in the *Lyttleton Times*:

We anticipate that the tour of the MCC will have a splendid inspirational effect on New Zealand cricket. The veteran captain of the English team has a reputation which is something to conjure with in international cricketing circles . . . . Other cricketers have made more sensational scores under favourable conditions, but the achievements of MacLaren when everything was wrong – the wicket bad, the bowling deadly, and the score hopelessly against his side – have won him a warm niche in the hearts of all who love cricket, and who cherish the British tradition that it is 'dogged as does it' . . . . A cardinal point of MacLaren's creed is that cricket ought to be pre-served as a purely amateur sport. His utterances on the subject, especially some references to professionalism in Britain, have occas-ioned some perturbation in English cricketing circles, but in Australia and New Zealand, where we are not troubled with professionalism in cricket to any great extent, and do not wish the commercialisation of the game to make headway, his remarks have been accepted with cordial approbation . . . . We feel sure that the Englishmen ought to be able to teach us a good deal about the game, and under so notable a schoolmaster as MacLaren we can take a licking and feel that it is an honour to be licked.

Canterbury's cricket had been at a lowish ebb over the previous few years, so a licking certainly seemed the likely outcome of this match anyway. Their captain was Billy Patrick, remembered by Dan Reese as 'a clever tactician and able leader'. Reese also recalled the start of New Zealand's match against Victoria at Melbourne in 1913-14: 'Patrick and Hemus opened our innings. When facing McDonald, the former snicked his first ball to Armstrong at first slip; he dropped it! His second ball went to second slip; he dropped it! Patrick left the third ball alone and it hit the top of the off stump! Was a 0 ever more fully deserved?' This season, however, he had already made two centuries in club cricket and the local press was talking of him as a possible New Zealand captain. Another survivor of the 1913-14 tour was Don Sandman, who, 'if he could have been restrained a little', Dan Reese thought, 'would have become a very good batsman'. Characteristically, a score of 12 not out in only his second first-class innings had comprised two sixes off Warwick Armstrong. Sandman was also a leg-break and googly bowler of considerable skill. Opening the batting for Canterbury was Rupert Vivian de Renzy Worker, a sound left-hander who had been coached at Auckland Grammar School by Shacklock (who in the course of his time in New Zealand coached in all four big cities). Worker, a teacher by profession, had previously played for Auckland before moving south. His opening partner was Roger Blunt, the province's sole national representative at this stage of the series. A very sound and determined accumulator of runs, though not unstylish, Blunt was by 1922 clearly becoming a major batsman, with his only weakness being an over-fondness for the cut. He had been born at Durham in 1900, but came as a baby to New Zealand on his father being appointed Professor of Modern Languages at the University of

Canterbury. His captain at Christ's College for two years was Tom Lowry and he himself made his provincial debut at the age of seventeen as much as a leg-break bowler as a batsman. A cool, self-contained young man, he had played for New Zealand against the Australians in 1920-21 and was unlikely to be overawed by reputations.

Freeman and Tyldesley were omitted for the third consecutive match; Maclean had injured his hand in Wanganui; and Hill-Wood played even though he was, according to Pope, still suffering from headaches as a result of an attack of yellow jaundice in England. On Saturday the 23rd, MCC took the Canterbury attack apart at Lancaster Park: Wilkinson scored a century, but the innings of the day was Chapman's 183 in 135 minutes. The local response to 'this young giant with the curly hair and pleasant smile' was understandably ecstatic:

Wristy, sweeping drives that possessed power with the minimum of effort, and graceful shots all round the wicket, revealed the artist. Perhaps his best stroke was a sparkling square-cut – an affair of the wrists that Read and Sandman found expensive. He has some beautiful leg shots too. And his driving is splendid. At all times his batting was sound and crisp. It was perfectly timed. In his most forceful play, Chapman suggested a reserve of power. And also was that feature marked in his back play. Batsmen capable of such offensive back play as Chapman's are rare. Very seldom was he really on the defensive. But mostly it was in forward play that he indulged his abilities. In this he used his great height and reach, and his strokes, quick and sure, represented a perfect co-ordination of timing and graceful effort.

Or as the headline of another paper put it: 'Will Trumper's Mantle Fall On Chapman?' Later on the first day, Geoffrey Wilson came in at 357 for 5 and struggled for over an hour to reach double figures, causing some ironical comment from the ring. MacLaren declared overnight at 454 for 6, not batting himself. Canterbury then batted poorly on Christmas Day, succumbing to Gibson and Hartley for 181 (Sandman a relatively restrained 43), before later that day and into Tuesday some honour was salvaged as Blunt (174) and Worker (65) achieved an opening partnership of 208. But then came a remarkable spell of bowling by Gibson (8 for 57), leaving

Canterbury all out for 295 and MCC running out comfortable winners by eight wickets. The star fieldsman over the final two days was predictable: 'Chapman, at forward cover, astonished the crowd [of several thousand] at times by the way he went after and saved boundary shots. His returns from balls that he had to chase were little short of remarkable and gained him frequent applause.' Though similarly full of praise for Gibson's bowling, the *Sun* was sad enough about Canterbury's batsmen: 'With two or three exceptions, they played either nervous or uncultured cricket: cricket which must have made some of the old-timers squirm. The rough-and-ready, self-taught batsman is out of his depth in the big games nowadays, when sound defence and versatility in strokes are absolutely essential weapons.'

During Canterbury's first innings, on Christmas Day afternoon, the captain joined W. Hayes with the score 53 for 3: 'Patrick knew little about the first ball from Calthorpe. A leg-bye gave Patrick the opportunity of facing Gibson, and then the earth quaked!' It did indeed, as Ferguson recorded in his scoring book: 'Earthquake, 3.04 p.m. Grandstand is rocking. Titchmarsh has difficulty in picking up the ball.' Elsewhere in Christchurch the spire of the Anglican Cathedral began swaying and the bells were set ringing, while the scene at Lancaster Park was not without drama, as the *Sun* recorded:

That portion of the crowd who were not in the stands appeared to enjoy the experience of the earthquake. Those in the stands obviously did not share this point of view. The swaying of the buildings and the creaking of the huge timbers were not exactly calculated to exercise a soothing effect.

When the ground quaked, play promptly stopped and was not resumed for three minutes. The visitors seemed interested and, with the crowd on the embankment, devoted attention to several swaying chimneys and tank stands. The big chimney at the Waltham gasworks was noticeably moving.

The members' stand is built high, and it developed a nautical roll. Timbers creaked as though they were masts in a gale. If anyone enjoyed the 'rocking of the boat', there were no cries of pleasure. The only sounds other than the protesting timbers were the shrill chirping of birds above, who left their nests in the ceiling and fluttered wildly

B. J. Kortlang and E. H. L. Bernau

against the wire-netting in an endeavour to get out.

Below, no one moved. Many, doubtless, wanted to, but pride forbade. On the eastern stand, a ground-floor affair, one woman ran out, white and shaking. A man followed, to attend to her.

The quake lasted for some sixty five seconds and, as Ferguson recalled, MacLaren shouted across to his wife to leave the members' stand. Maclean, who was in the pavilion at the time, recalls the ground appearing to be in waves. Play, once it restarted, was understandably quiet, with no addition to the total for seven minutes except for a leg-bye. After a while, Calthorpe had Patrick caught for 18, to make the score 81 for 4: 'The newcomer was J. Young, and he played an over. "Shake it up!" came from the crowd.' Last word, however, went as usual to MacLaren. Asked afterwards if he had ever before taken part in a game interrupted by an earthquake, he replied: 'No, never before – and I don't want another!'

Less dramatically, while all this was going on, Wellington and Auckland were playing at the Basin Reserve the first Plunket Shield match of the season, over four days from Saturday to Wednesday. Since the previous season the old challenge system had been replaced by a league basis, with each of the four major provinces (Auckland, Wellington, Canterbury, and Otago) meeting the others once, with matches to be played to a finish. For Wellington, Kortlang came in as a late replacement for Wanganui's injured Holland (major associations being allowed to select players from adjacent minor ones, though often reluctant to do so). It proved to be a well-contested match of sizeable crowds and heaps of runs: Wellington 435 (Bernau 117, Kortlang 113, Allcott 5 for 92) and 396 (Collins 116, McGirr 95); Auckland 386 (Dacre 145) and 337 (Snedden 88). The new man established himself as a favourite on the first day: 'Kortlang delighted the crowd with aggressive play all round the wicket, and showed a partiality for shots past third man and the well-known Australian hook.' In the second innings he made 53, despite a long-standing knee injury forcing him at one point to be carried off. By contrast, Hiddleston had an indifferent game, and not only with the bat, as the *New Zealand Times* commented: 'His fielding was on the heavy side. He ought to try and train off about two stones of weight, and then perhaps he will find that he can bat as well as ever.' 'Burwood' of the Wellington *Dominion* was especially impressed by the footwork of Dacre and McGirr: 'Neither believe in the time-worn English adage that a batsman's foot must be always in his crease. New Zealand batsmen, with very few exceptions, still cling to the belief that the wicketkeeper has them almost as much at his mercy as the bowler.' Dacre was in fact dropped on the second day by Kortland off a skier, but the fielder subsequently excused himself by saying that he had been hindered by the earthquake. There seems also to have been a certain amount of needle in this match, springing from the moment when Kortlang was caught and bowled low down by Snedden, but, with the elderly umpire unsighted, declined to walk. Dacre, some years later, recalled what happened afterwards: 'I was fielding square-leg to Allcott when Herb McGirr hit one on the half-volley to me. I smothered the ball so quickly that Dick Rowntree, our keeper, threw up his arms and cried out, "Well caught, Sis!" Poor McGirr had to go, to make up for one or two of his pals who had really been caught before.' Statistically, the match aggregate of 1,554 runs was the highest at that time for a first-class match outside Australia. Unusually for Wellington, the wicket was made from local soil, taken (as with the wicket for the coming 'Test') from the city's new Prince of Wales Park. And: 'When stumps were drawn, with Auckland 108 runs in the rear, the wicket was inspected and found to be quite sound, except for the two small pockets made by Kortlang's plunge at two yorkers.'

The English team arrived in Wellington on Wednesday morning, as the match was finishing. They were without Hartley, who had stayed behind on South Island for a fishing holiday. New Zealand, however, suffered the greater blows, as it emerged that not only had Shepherd gone down with a bad attack of flu which made him doubtful for the 'Test' on Saturday, but also that, in the match against Wellington, Rowntree had aggravated an injury he had received against MCC to such an extent that he was definitely unavailable. The selectors sounded out Wellington's wicket-keeper, A. Cate, but since his job involved him sharing duties with Stan Brice, he was compelled to rule himself out. In some desperation, then, the position was given to J. W. Condliffe, who in recent years had mostly confined himself to club cricket in Wellington, but before the war had played for both Otago and New Zealand. In the English camp, the team on Thursday morning put in a couple of hours' practice at the Basin, during which MacLaren 'kept a fatherly eye on the young players, and every now and then would stop and point out some fault in style'. He also took the opportunity to sound off to the press about one aspect of the tour to date:

So far he had not played on a good wicket in New Zealand . . . . The state of the wickets was not due in any way to the work of the groundsmen, but to the amount of sandy material in the soil. He had been told by the custodian of the Basin Reserve that the wicket had been watered during the [Plunket Shield] match with the consent of the captains, but he himself would never allow such a thing to happen. It was against the principles of cricket as they were understood in England. Watering the wicket did not give the bowlers a chance, as it made a wearing wicket into a first-class one. He knew from his thirty years' experience in first-class cricket that once a wicket began to show signs of wear it never improved with rolling, and the only way in which it would improve would be by watering.

It was stern stuff, born at least partly out of MacLaren's aggravating experience at Sydney. But before he started to implement his English principles, the tourists were given the day off on Friday to relax before the big match: 'Mr and Mrs Ian Duncan organised a delightful motor picnic for the visitors to their stud farm at Waikanae. The party were taken in cars over a terrible road, certainly, but the beautiful view of the native bush compensated for the defects of the road.'

As the match approached, the local press was not altogether sanguine about New Zealand's chances of putting up a good show. The *New Zealand Times* was alarmed at 'the meagre quality of the bowling' and in particular at the way the pace bowling depended too heavily on the veteran Brice: 'Although Brice has worked hard for a good many years, it is idle to deny the fact that on good sound wickets he is, and has been, a plain bowler.' And the gloomy preview continued: 'If the fielding was of high quality one would not be so pessimistic, but as the sprinkling of colts who are good fields does not outweigh the badness of that of the veterans, the bowlers need not look there for much assistance.' It was indeed a well-seasoned team that New Zealand was putting into the field, with only McLeod and Garrard not having played before at a high representative level. What it desperately lacked, though, was proper match practice; the recent Plunket Shield match had been a help, but hardly complete preparation. Still, the moment was at hand and public interest in the coming encounter ran at a high level. 'New Zealand has made many bids for international cricket fame', the *Dominion* somewhat wryly declared on the morning of the match, before going on:

On the whole, the record of New Zealand international cricket is necessarily a record of failures against superior opponents; but, although the Dominion has been the under-dog throughout the piece, progress has been maintained, when it is remembered what strides Australian cricket has made. One may be pardoned therefore for looking with confidence to the result of the first Test match against MacLaren's team, which commences today on the historic Basin Reserve, where New Zealand cricket has been cradled.

·4·

*MacLaren survives run out — MacLaren majestic —
MacLaren declares — MacLaren's safe hands —
MacLaren's match*

In accordance with his usual practice, MacLaren named his
team on the morning of the match. Freeman was included, but
not Tyldesley; Hill-Wood was still not a hundred per cent; and
Hartley had gone fishing. For New Zealand, Shepherd played,
though not yet properly recovered from his bout of flu. With
MacLaren sticking firm to his line that the wicket was to be
tended strictly in accordance with the laws of cricket, the toss
took on an especial importance. MacLaren won it and naturally
elected to bat, sending in Titchmarsh and Wilkinson to open.
The crowd at the start of play numbered several thousand and,
in the words of the *New Zealand Free Lance*, 'it was really beautiful
weather', though 'a cold, searching southerly drove many people
out of the stand on to the sun-warmed grassy slopes outside'.

The openers made a circumspect start against the bowling of
Brice and Allcott, with Titchmarsh in particular 'careful to a
degree – just stolid batting with an occasional leg-glance and a
gentle pat through the slips'. Wilkinson had reached 17 when
he pulled Brice to leg: 'Collins threw himself headlong and
made a magnificent catch, but winded himself as he crashed to
the ground, but soon recovered.' Two more wickets quickly
followed: Titchmarsh fell for 22 to Brice's canny use of the cross
wind, leg-before as he tried to hit a swerving ball to leg; and

72

Chapman was 'beautifully caught by Allcott, one-handed, at second slip' for 1, 'playing back to a good-length ball from Brice, which apparently swung away'. Calthorpe and Wilson then fashioned a useful partnership: Calthorpe took most of the bowling and scored at a steady rate, though should have been stumped by Condliffe; while Wilson strung together a dozen singles, almost all to leg, and was 'mildly barracked by the crowd for his lack of enterprise'. Coming up to lunch, however, Snedden had the Yorkshire captain caught behind and the adjournment was immediately made, with the score 108 for 4 and New Zealand on top.

MacLaren's appearance with Calthorpe afterwards was 'the signal for an enthusiastic outburst of applause from the large crowd, and it was continued until the MCC captain took his place at the crease'. MacLaren quietly defended the final ball of Snedden's over and was soon down at the other end: 'He glanced a delivery from Brice to fine leg and attempted a run, but smart fielding by Allcott caused the batsman to quickly regain his crease. Condliffe fumbled slightly, and MacLaren was safe.' Such was the report in the *Evening Post*, though the Press Association report identified the fine leg as Hiddleston, while according to the *Dominion* the throw was 'execrable' and Condliffe 'could readily be excused for not taking it'. MacLaren then got off the mark, but was only on 1 when Garrard, in the process of bowling five successive maidens, had Calthorpe caught behind for 63. Lowry then joined his captain and, though he also started quietly, the balance of the match then perceptibly changed as both batsmen began to seize the initiative from the bowlers. The fieldsmen were still on their toes and 'doing good work in keeping the runs down', at least until 'Hiddleston at cover badly missed MacLaren's stroke for a boundary'. Soon afterwards, with the score past the 150 mark, MacLaren 'got hold of Garrard and sent him over the eastern boundary for six, without any apparent effort'. It was a stunning stroke that made a deep impression on everyone present. 'A hook forward of square-leg, which went from the bat across the boundary like a shot from the gun', was another paper's description; while the *Dominion*'s correspondent felt that 'it seemed almost cruel for MacLaren to have extracted a sixer from the ball Garrard sent

Titchmarsh and Calthorpe batting in the First 'Test'

down, that bounced near the middle of the pitch'. It must have been a flat hit, for according to Wilkinson's account, Blunt, fielding at (presumably fairly wide) mid-on, jumped up and almost caught the ball. One of the spectators in the crowd was Jack Gregg, who sixty years later recalled of that hit, for all its power almost a flick, 'We just opened our mouths.'

MacLaren reached his half century in almost even time and the pace of scoring further accelerated, before a good break ball from Allcott defeated Lowry, who had scored 54 and put on 127 with MacLaren in sixty three minutes. Brand then provided solid if somewhat passive support while MacLaren continued to play his celebrated strokes. Soon after tea, with his score in the nineties, he 'just missed being run out, the spectators applauding loudly as he reached his crease'. Then, amidst more

74

loud applause from a crowd numbering 6,500 by the middle of
the afternoon, a four off Garrard took him to his century, made
in 130 minutes. The even tenor of the scoring continued, though
Shepherd bowled a useful spell in which he 'had MacLaren
thinking' – but perhaps only about the keen wind, for about this
time he sent out for his neck wrap. Brand finally fell to Shepherd
for 33 and was replaced by Maclean, who right from the start hit
about the bowling with considerable vigour. He was lucky with
one or two skiers that fell close to hand, but he and MacLaren
went undefeated through the last hour, with MacLaren, though
visibly tiring, even having the energy to take an all-run four off
Shepherd. The score at stumps was 432 for 7, with MacLaren
162 not out and Maclean 55 not out. MacLaren had been
batting for three and three-quarter hours and received 'a great
reception on returning to the pavilion'.

The press gave the New Zealand team pretty much a lashing

Archie's Last Stand: MacLaren and Maclean going out to bat on the second morning

for its first-day performance. Brice 'was splendid for the first 10 overs, but after that never looked like taking a wicket', though according to one paper he ricked his thigh in going for a ball soon after lunch. Allcott 'was dangerous in patches', but 'kept the ball a yard too short most of the time'. Garrard was the pick of the bowlers, but 'has certainly lost his former quick nip off the pitch'. Smith, 'although he kept the batsmen playing him, did not look difficult enough to cause the batsmen any uneasiness' and 'should have been taken off long before he was'. Similarly disappointing, especially as the day wore on, was the fielding: 'The ground-work and returns to the wicket were slow, and far too many strokes were stopped by the foot, which is not what one expects in a test match.' Hiddleston, although making some good stops in the covers, was particularly patchy and 'had to put up with some barracking from the crowd at times'. As for Smith, he 'at times seemed too lazy to stop a ball and often put his foot out for the ball in the most casual manner'. The honourable exception to the rule was Blunt, whose 'work in the country was

a real treat'. Condliffe did not do too badly behind the stumps, but he was still 'far below Rowntree's form'. Some of the hardest brick-bats were reserved for Snedden as captain: 'The field was never placed to the best advantage and the bowlers were badly managed'. The *Dominion* added: 'Who that saw it will forget how MacLaren stepped back from the crease and calmly surveyed the nine traps elaborately set for him, and then proceeded to clout the ball to the boundary through the huge gap between cover-point and the bowler?'

On Saturday evening 'an impromptu little dance was got up for the visitors at Mrs Morice's', while 'on Sunday, another glorious day, the *Janie Seddon* conveyed the visitors first across the blue and sparkling waters to Somes Island – now so happily purged of Huns – and then on to Lowry Bay to the residence of their host, Sir Francis Bell, for afternoon tea'. Play was resumed on New Year's Day in front of a crowd of almost 5,000. 'The wicket was in good order, though dry, and there were some expressions of opinion as to the damage Freeman would do with the ball on such a wicket.' First, though, MacLaren and Maclean continued their partnership, quickly taking the score up to 499 before Maclean was caught off a skier at mid-off, having made

84 in ninety minutes. Freeman joined MacLaren, who was on 194 and had earlier given a couple of near chances as well as avoiding a run out only by virtue of Snedden fumbling the ball as the batsmen went through for a dangerous single. Now, however, there were no more alarms: 'A single to the veteran made the MCC score 500 for 377 minutes, and with a four to mid-off and another single MacLaren achieved his objective. He thereupon declared.' The total was 505 for 8 and 'cheering broke into a perfect salvo of applause as MacLaren mounted the steps of the pavilion'. His score of 200 not out had taken just under four and a half hours and had featured twenty eight 4s in addition to the memorable six off Garrard.

In reply, it took Hiddleston until the second ball of the innings to put away Gibson for four, but one run later he fell to a smart catch by MacLaren at slip. Other disasters followed before lunch: Blunt 'sent an easy catch to Chapman at cover-point'; Smith was 'thrown out by Titchmarsh in attempting an impossible run for a short stroke to leg'; and Snedden played on to 'a particularly good ball from Gibson, which swung in from the off'. Shepherd and Collins then stayed together for a while, but as the afternoon progressed it was clear that the New Zealand batsmen had no real answer to the spin of Freeman, who finished with 5 for 114 off 40 overs. Garrard and McLeod both made some vigorous strokes, while Allcott's 38 not out was a stoical effort. McLeod remembers how, before the innings, he and Garrard were approached by Freeman and told that, because they were both playing for New Zealand for the first time, he (Freeman) would give them each an early full toss; apparently McLeod missed his, but Garrard hit a grateful four. Last man in was Brice, who was dropped first ball by MacLaren and made a few good clumps before, 'in essaying another big hit, tipped the ball into the slips, and MacLaren was ready'. The home team had scored 222 in 192 minutes (80.2 overs bowled) and were asked to follow on.

The second innings got off to a sluggish start; after ten overs, the score was 2 for 0 when Gibson bowled Shepherd for what MacLaren later described as 'the best duck he'd ever seen'. Hiddleston joined Blunt and they took the score to 49 for 1 at stumps. During the night a little rain fell and MacLaren was asked by a reporter the next morning how the wicket was going, to which he replied laughingly: 'It's not going at all. It is holding very well and is a good wicket.' The weather was delightful and there was gathered 'a good muster all round the ground', but New Zealand, once Blunt had gone fairly early on, batted abjectly against Gibson and Freeman. Soon after he had been painfully struck on the thigh by a straight drive from Snedden, Hiddleston went the same way as Blunt, caught at slip by MacLaren, though 'the batsman was surprised at the decision, thinking evidently that he had played the ball to the ground first'. Then with the score still on 72, Smith 'made a desperate lunge at the second ball Gibson sent him, and it flew to the hands of Chapman at cover-point', completing his pair and a generally unhappy match. Yet worse was to come; Collins tamely placed Gibson into the hands of Titchmarsh at short mid-on (72 for 5); and Snedden, 'trying to spoon Freeman to leg, played the ball on to his wicket' (76 for 6). Garrard and McLeod managed some token resistance, but Freeman then dismissed McLeod, Allcott, and Condliffe with the score immobile at 92. As one report put it in Miltonic phrase, the wickets were falling 'like autumn leaves in Vallambrosa' as Brice stepped out for the final fling: 'He began with a four to the boundary, which drew forth mirthful cheers. He followed it with another smite to the boundary. (More hilarious cheering.) Then came a two, another four, and a six over the fence into the crowd. (Tumultuous cheering.) The English captain was induced to put another man on the boundary away out near the screen, but after a couple of singles Brice played one into MacLaren's safe hands and the innings was at an end.' The total was 127, Gibson and Freeman had shared the wickets, and the match was over a quarter of an hour before lunch.

Defeat by an innings and 156 runs left the pundits with cruel things to say about New Zealand's batsmen as well as bowlers. According to the Dunedin *Evening Star*'s reporter, 'the dominant factors in the downfall were the fine bowling of Gibson and Freeman, the good fielding, and the nervousness of the batsmen'. This question of nerves was a theme common to all the inquests. 'On taking their stand at the crease the players "had the wind up"', asserted the *Evening Post*; while 'Touchline' of the *New*

Zealand Free Lance reckoned that '"stage fright" primarily, and a too exalted idea of the quality of the Englishmen's bowling, accounted for the retirement of many of New Zealand's batsmen'. H.C. Watson of the *Sun* pointed out that for most of the final morning Freeman's only deep fielder was placed at long-leg, yet the batsmen still failed to get down the wicket and drive. The *New Zealand Times* agreed (though mentioning Shepherd as an exception): 'There was too much playing back to the slow bowling. Many of the New Zealand team hardly moved their feet at all. In this country the true value of a slow bowler is never realised, and very few batsmen attempt to play one in a scientific manner.' Some critics, however, did put at least part of the blame on the wicket, especially in the light of MacLaren's pre-match refusal to allow the curator, 'Budge' Brewer, to do anything in the form of overnight rolling or watering that would improve it for the second and third days. 'The wicket had the top roughened considerably as the result of England's long score', stated one paper, 'and the bowlers were able to spin the ball very quickly.' Even discounting MacLaren's opinion, there was probably not all that much truth to this explanation. Certainly, the correspondent of the *Press* thought that on the last day 'the English bowlers got some assistance from a pitch that was beginning to wear, but it was still a good pitch'. Few if any of the New Zealand batsmen had had recent match practice against top-class spin bowling and they would surely have been struggling on almost any wicket. While as for their collective failure against Gibson, there was at least one honourable precedent.

Yet once the post-mortems had been delivered, digested, and duly filed away, what lingered was neither the state of the wicket nor the sad procession of local batsmen, but instead the historic splendour of MacLaren's innings. 200 not out at the age of 51, even against somewhat indifferent bowling, was a feat to be savoured, not least by MacLaren himself as the telegrams of congratulation poured in . It was not a flawless innings – in particular he seems to have missed quite a lot going down the leg side – but it was undoubtedly a notable one, as all the contemporary reports make abundantly clear. Thus the *Dominion* recorded how his best-known stroke was still in good working order: 'He gave flashes of his old-time judgement in hooking every ball that could be hooked; yet rarely did he play under the ball, which cannoned to the turf and sped to the pickets at a great pace.' While according to the *Evening Star*'s correspondent, 'he gave a finished display of stylish strokes all round the wicket, his pull stroke and drive past forward cover bringing him most of his runs'. Perhaps the best technical description of MacLaren's innings was in the *Sun*, which, after noting that his 'best scoring strokes were hard forward shots past mid-off and through the covers, skilfully-placed leg-glances, and well-placed forcing shots between mid-on and short-leg', went on: 'Many times, when an attempt was made to block his on-side play, he deliberately lifted the ball over the heads of the in-field. His footwork on all his shots was an object lesson. Compared with the rest of the Englishmen, he was as a master among his pupils.' The surviving witnesses would not dissent: 'graceful' is Gregg's epithet for the innings as a whole; while another youthful spectator, R. W. Archer, recalls MacLaren's cutting, his seeming 'wrists of steel', and the increasing desperation of the fielders, quite unable to get him out. One of those fielders was McLeod, who remembers with some wryness what he calls 'a spectacular innings'. But the best tribute of all was paid nearer the time, by an unknown member of MacLaren's team, perhaps Calthorpe. According to the account usually quoted, he simply said, 'Until we saw this innings we never knew what batting is.'

MacLaren after his innings

·5·

Within hours of the match ending at the Basin Reserve, the New Zealand side was announced for the Second 'Test' beginning at Christchurch on Friday the 5th. Brice, Smith, McLeod, and Hiddleston were dropped, being replaced by Dacre, Lambert, Bernau, and McGirr, with Sandman as twelfth man. 'Bill' Bernau was a twenty six year old whose family came from Hawke's Bay; and, like Lowry, he had been coached as a boy by Jack Board. He was a somewhat variable medium-fast left-arm bowler and a hard-hitting batsman, owing his selection to his good all-round performance for Wellington against Auckland. The same applied to Herb McGirr, who had played a little for Wellington before the war, but was now emerging as one of the 'greats' in Wellington's cricket history. He was an utterly enthusiastic, combative sort of cricketer, who bowled untiringly somewhere above medium and as a batsman was usually on the attack. All four new selections were approved by the critics, above all on the grounds that they made for a more youthful, energetic team. Smith was generally reckoned to be past it, while as for Brice, even the *Evening Post* in Wellington accepted that 'his active service now covers a very long period' and that perhaps he likewise fell into that category. The same paper added, however, that 'McLeod must have been a hard man to drop, as his knock for 22 in the first innings was of the right type, and he was shaping well in the second innings until use of his brains was neglected in playing the "googly" bowler.' Hiddleston was a special case: his 38 had been top score in the second innings, but it seems that the selectors dropped him because of his erratic fielding and perhaps also his weight. In addition to the actual changes that were made, the *Dominion* thought that Sandman for Collins would have been a good move; while the *New Zealand Times* also supported the candidature of Sandman and would have liked to see him coming in for Snedden, adding darkly that 'the desirability of having a player as selector is open to question'.

However, the major criticism of the team, voiced in all quarters, concerned the non-inclusion of Kortlang. In fact, at a meeting of the NZCC's management committee held on Tuesday at 2.15 at Sir Francis Bell's Private Office, Parliamentary Buildings, C. G. Wilson attended on behalf of the Wellington Cricket Association and stated that Kortlang had informed him that he had arrived in the Dominion during June 1922. Wilson added 'that he had proposed Kortlang as a member of the Wellington Association at its annual meeting held in September, and that Kortlang had given him to understand that it was his intention, as far as he knew at the present time, to leave the Dominion again in March'. In the light of that information it was decided that Kortlang was not eligible. Bell then issued a statement to the press, which began by acknowledging 'that Mr Kortlang is a very fine cricketer and one with whom all cricketers would be glad to play for or against', but went on:

What we felt was that we had invited the MCC to send a team to play against New Zealand, and we could not feel certain that Mr Kortlang, who is an able cricketer in another country and whose present visit to New Zealand has been of short duration, came within the definition of a New Zealander for the purpose of representing the Dominion at cricket. We felt sure that the MCC would not object to the inclusion of any player selected by New Zealand. With that in mind we were even more careful to limit the New Zealand team to men whose qualifications as New Zealanders were undoubted. We felt that New

Zealanders would agree that it was far better to avoid any question in the event for which we still hope – that New Zealand will win at least one of the Tests.

The statement ended by noting that this decision did not affect Kortlang's right to play in Plunket Shield matches, since he had fulfilled the required six months residential qualification. The reaction of 'Touchline' was typical of the general dismay: 'I consider the action of the NZCC an unmerited slap in the face of one of the finest fellows and keenest cricketers I have met.' The Wellington press was quickly talking to the man himself:

Kortlang is surprised at the decision of the Council. He stated that in all his experience in various parts of the world he had never known such a course of action in barring a man who practically by birth was entitled to play. He admitted that to some extent he was 'a bird of passage'. But New Zealand had been his permanent home since 1919. His business necessitated a good deal of travelling, but what other men who were travellers had been debarred on account of residential qualifications? Although he was born in Australia, his mother was a New Zealander. He first came to the Dominion in 1912, and he was here for eight months in the following year. He then went to South Africa and afterwards to New York, subsequently going to the war. He returned here from America in 1919, and since that time he has been absent for only two or three short periods of three or four months. At the commencement of the present cricket season there was a likelihood that he would play in Christchurch, and he had actually had practices in that city without having any undertaking to play for a club. He mentioned, incidentally, that after one practice at the nets in the southern city he had been offered a place in a third eleven. His business, however, brought him back to Wellington, and he immediately informed an official of the Wellington club that he would be able to play from December 8 [when rain in fact washed out play], having recovered fairly well from his war injuries.

The *Evening Post* on Thursday the 4th provided an interesting postscript to this interview: 'The manager of the house at which Kortlang is residing stated today that during the past ten years Kortlang had been, on and off, a resident of the house, and when making any trips abroad he had left his goods in the building. Other residents of the same place stated that they had known Kortlang to have been a resident there at various times during the past twelve years.'

The Kortlang controversy apart, preparations for the Second 'Test' were more or less straightforward. The teams travelled to Christchurch overnight by ferry steamer on Tuesday, with the only serious question being whether an old knee injury of MacLaren's which had flared up again at the Basin would allow him to play. Eventually, on Pope's advice, he decided to stand down, with the result that Hartley replaced him as captain, the only change made. On Thursday, while the New Zealanders put in some 'solid practice' at Lancaster Park, the tourists 'were entertained at a shooting party at Hororata'. The match began on Friday, but, 'for some reason best known to the authorities in Christchurch' (according to the *Evening Post*), play did not start until two o'clock. Perhaps the reason was tacitly referred to by the *Press*: 'Considering that there was only a partial holiday in town, the attendance was very good, the sum of £226 being taken at the gates.' Saturday was still better: 'The crowd was variously estimated at from six to eight thousand. It was the biggest cricket crowd seen in Christchurch for many years, and it contributed at the gates no less a sum than £490.' Even on Monday there was a fair-sized crowd, paying £151 at the gate, at an average of just under two bob a head. One of those present was the Wellington Cricket Association's treasurer, J. Reid, who was later asked about his time in Christchurch: 'Public interest in the game is very keen, and there was a large attendance at the Test match. I was particularly struck by the way it was being discussed in hotels, shops, tramcars, and other places by most unlikely people.'

The main reason for this enthusiasm was no doubt the much-improved performance of the national team. Snedden won the toss, Collins square cut Gibson for four first ball, and New Zealand compiled a total of 375 in only 259 minutes. Collins scored an excellent century and Shepherd an attractive 66, while of the newcomers Dacre made 45, Lambert 33, and McGirr 40 not out. The fielding stayed good, though three times in quick succession Maclean conceded four byes to Freeman, with each time Titchmarsh being engaged in a fruitless chase from which 'the crowd derived considerable amusement'. One paper was favourably struck by the way in which no appeal was made by the English side in the field 'unless by those in a position to have reason that the appeal is legitimate'. In reply, after Wilson and Titchmarsh had both scratched around and gone cheaply, Wilkinson, Chapman, and Lowry all batted freely, so that with rather over an hour still remaining of Saturday's play the MCC score was 272 for 7. At which point the eighth wicket pair dug in: '"Good old Colonel", came a voice from the crowd, as Hartley just stopped a low one from Bernau. "Go on, Colonel", and "Get into it, Brand", was encouragingly shouted. At this stage Garrard bowled a maiden, and every stroke of the batsmen was ironically cheered.' Over the next hour the batsmen 'showed great patience, but the crowd did not, and most unmercifully chaffed the "Colonel"'. At stumps the score was 329 for 7 and on Monday morning MCC finished with a total of 384, made in 349 minutes, with Hartley 60 not out. McGirr and Bernau each took four wickets. New Zealand then batted briskly to reach 270 for 8 in 168 minutes, with Snedden (a duck in the first innings) and Dacre each scoring 58. Snedden declared at tea, setting MCC a target of 262 in just under two hours. Watching events was a Wellington enthusiast who sent his account to the *Evening Post*:

The English order is as before, and Titchmarsh and Wilson send up twenty in twenty minutes against McGirr and Bernau. Allcott replaces Bernau, and Wilson brings up thirty in thirty minutes. Not fast enough, but perhaps they are just feeling their way for a start. Thirty five in thirty five minutes, and McGirr off in favour of Garrard, whose first over is a maiden. Allcott bowls another, and one begins to feel that the New Zealand bowling must be pretty good after all, when the Englishmen, always out for the win, are so quiet. Even a full toss from Garrard fails to tempt Wilson. 'Oh!' sigh the crowd as Titchmarsh gets Allcott away in the slips between Blunt and McGirr, but it was too high to be a chance. Still a run a minute, and the rate of scoring requires increasing as the minutes fly. Snedden replaces Allcott, and the crowd cheer as Wilson gets a single. Well they might, although they did not know it at the moment, for Titchmarsh hits the next ball into Blunt's hands, and the first wicket is down. 212 wanted, and seventy minutes to go. Wilkinson is next in. Surely he will liven it up a bit. He is playing Garrard with his legs, so that doesn't look much like it. An odd single or two – they are not after the runs evidently . . .

Collins caught and bowled by Brand for 102

Calthorpe bowled by McGirr for 14

Nor were they. At the close MCC were 145 for 5, Wilkinson 41 not out, and the match was left drawn. That evening Hartley, Hill-Wood, Blunt, Wilkinson, and Chapman all attended 'the dance held at Dixieland, to celebrate the close of the Test match', with music provided by Sutherland's Jazz Band.

The refurbished New Zealand team had acquitted itself more than creditably, though Condliffe's wicket-keeping came in for some criticism and the *Dominion* also suggested that Patrick would make a better captain than Snedden, who, it argued, should have used Bernau and McGirr (tired though they presumably were) to break up the crucial Hartley-Brand partnership on Saturday afternoon. The major broadside, though, was that directed by the *Sun* at the English batting, which, with the exception of Chapman, was described as 'not strong in strokes, rarely enterprising, and studiedly conventional'. A disenchanted, and not altogether logical, editorial continued:

The English captain erred in tactics on Saturday afternoon and yesterday. On the Saturday the batsmen had their opponents almost entirely at their mercy, but, lacking imagination, they stonewalled. The policy adopted yesterday, when New Zealand declared, was equally unimaginative. Admittedly, it was impossible for such a batting side to get the runs in the time. It must also be admitted that the Englishmen ran practically no risk of being dismissed for a small score, even if they changed their methods or order of going in and opened their shoulders. Always the game is, or should be, greater than mere averages, and it is a pity the MCC skipper did not act on that principle. As a result, the concluding stages of the contest were funereal, and without a single redeeming feature. That kind of cricket can be seen in club matches every week without charge.

In a word, coming from a team that had 'the reputation of being a side that looked for the sporting side of cricket instead of the "records" side', it was, the *Sun* thought, a thoroughly disappointing performance.

In Wellington, meanwhile, Kortlang had been back in action on the Saturday, as the club match between Wellington and YMCA was resumed after a gap of three weeks. Kortlang scored 130, but Wellington still lost by 37 runs, with Bernau, otherwise engaged, unable to resume his innings. About this time Kortlang gave another interview: 'I am not a professional; I never have been, and never will be, though I have had some tempting offers in various parts of the world. My one object now is to help the young fellows. I am going to spend my time coaching the boys while I am here, and for the purpose I have been able to secure a wicket at the Basin Reserve.' Kortlang emphasised that he was not seeking a place in the New Zealand team: 'I have proved that by my actions. What I want is to get the youngsters there. As a kiddy I was kept down in Australia, and I realise the pain I felt in those days.' On the last day of the Christchurch match, the NZCC met to decide a couple of matters rather less contentious than the Kortlang question. One concerned the wish of the New South Wales Cricket Association to hire a band for the return match with MCC, but the NZCC declined to pay the cost of £23 16s 8d. And with regard to the other item, the NZCC likewise declined to accede to

Swan's request that it should stand the expense of afternoon teas for the members of the MCC team on the days when there was no match in progress.

On Tuesday the 9th (the day of Katherine Mansfield's death) the tourists caught an early train from Christchurch to the seaside resort of Timaru, where they were based for the match at nearby Temuka against a combined team representing Ashburton, South Canterbury, and North Otago. MacLaren decided not to travel south with the team, preferring to nurse his ricked knee and enjoy the hospitality of Arthur Sims at Opawa, a suburb of Christchurch. At the tiny but well-maintained Temuka ground, Ferguson related the historic deeds of Trumper and Crawford to an incredulous Chapman, who was only convinced when he was shown the old score book. The match itself on Tuesday and Wednesday, against a team that Maclean at the time thought would have been beaten by most village sides in England, was the most one-sided of the tour, with MCC winning at their ease by an innings and 204 runs. In the combined team's first innings of 52, Chapman opened the bowling, Tyldesley (playing his first match in New Zealand) took 5 for 19, and even Hill-Wood's notoriously slow slows secured 4 for 22. The following day it was Maclean's turn to open the bowling, though the main bowling honours in the course of the local team's 151 fell to those obdurate batsmen Wilson and Titchmarsh. Between innings, almost all the MCC batsmen contributed substantially to a total of 407, with Chapman and Calthorpe, comprising an unlikely last-wicket partnership, putting on 94 in barely half an hour. The main interest of the two days was sartorial and social. Those seen at Victoria Park on Tuesday included Miss Patty Macdonald ('pink and white striped fugi frock, black straw hat, with cire ribbon') and Mrs Gillies ('black silk stockingette jet embroidered, black velvet tricorn hat with glycerine quills'). Lunch for the teams on Wednesday, under the chairmanship of Beechey Macdonald, President of the South Canterbury Cricket Association, seems to have been a jolly affair: 'Mr Swan proposed the health of Mr Macdonald, and in a few racy remarks referred to the president's genial personality, and expressed to him the heartfelt thanks of the lady members of the party for Mr

Macdonald's overwhelming kindness to them. (Laughter and applause).' Swan may have tended rather to over-bowl himself in the speech-making department, as Wilkinson later put it, but at least he could extract a bit of turn.

The following day the team went on by train to Dunedin. According to a legend which has lingered ever since in New Zealand cricket circles, they arrived there to find that the professionals had been booked into the best hotel in town and the amateurs into an inferior one. If true, this may well have been the deliberate work of the local cricket association, but it could also easily have had something to do with Ferguson, to judge by the sequel to the Auckland episode with Swan that he records in his memoirs: 'As usual, I bided my time, and had the last laugh. Messrs MacLaren and Swan gave me the opportunity of acting as tour manager during the New Zealand games; from that moment on, I made it my business to get Ferguson, Freeman, and Tyldesley into the best rooms in the best hotels, leaving the rest of the players to make do with whatever was left after we were fixed up.' As requested by the team, there was no civic reception, but instead a mayoral welcome during luncheon on the Saturday of the match, when it fell to Hartley to make the reply: 'The team had come out here to do something more than play cricket. It desired to cement the bond of union between this, the farthest-down British possession, and the "funny old Mother Land". And, said the Colonel, the game of cricket did this jolly well.' Cricket apart, the team had a pretty hectic time during their weekend in Dunedin: on Friday they attended at His Majesty's Theatre the premiere of *Johnny, Get Your Gun*; on Saturday there was a dance in their honour; on Sunday the local Taxi Drivers' Association laid on a run out by motor to Sullivan's Dam; and on Monday there was another dance. The weather throughout the weekend was cold and showery, so the southern charm was doubly well exercised.

The actual match against Otago was, inevitably in the conditions, a low-scoring and fragmented affair. Early on Calthorpe sent back the Alloo brothers, Cecil and Arthur, for 2 and 5 respectively, but half centuries by Shepherd and Galland took Otago on Friday to a respectable total of 202. Of the fielders, 'Chapman was closely watched, and it was amusing to hear the

91

Chapman and Titchmarsh batting at Dunedin

chorus of astonished cries when he let one or two pass him.'
MCC's 222 in reply featured a typically attractive 53 by Chapman and a much more stolid 73 from Titchmarsh, compiled in
134 minutes. A Saturday crowd of several thousand (despite the
poor weather that wiped out the morning session) made 'some
feeble attempts at barracking', according to the *Evening Star*,
'but it rarely rose above the advice to "get a net", or "take your
time", or "go for 'em"'. Otago in fact had in their attack the
fastest bowler in New Zealand in the form of George Dickinson,
but he was an erratic performer and only bowled eight overs in
the whole match. The home team then made a poor fist of it in
the second innings, playing a series of rash strokes on an only
mildly difficult wicket that resulted in their being all out by
Monday morning for 129, with J. McMullan's 69 the only
significant score. MCC needed 110 and at one point were in
some trouble at 71 for 4, but Titchmarsh and Calthorpe saw
them home. Titchmarsh (37 not out in eighty seven minutes)
played the left-arm slow-mediums of Dan McBeath with especial
care and remained impervious to a further round of barracking.
He was 'ironically applauded every time he blocked a ball, but

he would not change his tactics'.

The *Otago Daily Times* on Monday morning was not impressed with the tourists' batting on the bitterly cold Saturday afternoon: 'The spectators expected to see cricket with some sparkle in it, but, apart from Chapman, there was no champagne, so to speak. The public were entitled to expect more interesting batting from a team which had travelled thousands of miles to try to educate us in the finer points of the game.' The *Sun* on Tuesday, with fresh ammunition at its disposal, expanded the attack:

MacLaren's team of English amateurs, with a sprinkling of professionals, was imported to this country for educational purposes. That is to say, the MCC side was brought to New Zealand to improve the local game: Dominion cricket has been in the doldrums for some time. The tour is an expensive matter for the NZCC, which will be lucky to balance accounts, we imagine. And we don't seem to be getting good value for our money. The visitors, with two or three exceptions, are not capable of teaching us much about batting or bowling; their fielding admittedly is in a higher class. But the team as a team is disappointing in quality, and disappointing, too, in its lack of enterprise. The Second Test provided a striking illustration of the truth of both assertions. One Dunedin critic at least felt moved to comment adversely on the slowness of some of the English batting in the match against Otago. At the conclusion of the game a correspondent of the *Sun* invited the English captain, J.C.Hartley, to express an opinion thereon. Having praised the provincial representatives and the wicket, the interviewee broke out into an attack on the 'adjectival people who wrote for the press in this country'. These graceless fellows were 'adjectivally ignorant of the game when they talked of slow cricket'. Dear, dear! We wonder who feels crushed. Mr Hartley's attitude is not only impertinent; it suggests that it is almost *lèse-majesté* for the MCC side to be criticised. That pose may be carried off successfully at home, but it assuredly will not do anywhere else.

The editorial then reiterated in more detail its criticisms of the previous week concerning the tame English batting in both innings of the Christchurch match, before winding up with its considered view of the tour to date:

The average rate of run-getting was funereal; the less said of the leadership the better. And this from amateurs who, we are told, are always prepared to play the game for the game's sake. It is performances of this kind which help us to understand more clearly the resounding failure of England in the international contests. English cricket sadly needs to be 'gingered up'. It is wanting in imagination, courage, and resource: virtues which are strongly characteristic of Australian play. On the MCC showing in the Second Test, when conditions were all in favour of the bat, it would pay New Zealand better to purchase its cricket tuition from Australian elevens instead of incurring heavy liabilities in bringing out English teams which can teach us little or nothing new in the two chief departments of the great summer game. That is our reply to Mr Hartley's ill-timed and petulant remarks. As a critic of the critics he scarcely shines. Apparently he requires to be reminded that the NZCC did not arrange the present tour with the object of giving a specified number of English cricketers a pleasant jaunt, all expenses paid, through several Australian states and this Dominion. If we who are footing the bill are not satisfied with services rendered, surely we are entitled to say so without running the risk of the 'adjectival' peevishness of one temporarily in authority?

In more moderate tones, the *Otago Daily Times* on Wednesday, reviewing the Dunedin match as a whole, singled out two English players for particular criticism. One was Titchmarsh:

'It must have been weary work to any but the keenest of keen enthusiasts watching his slow, plodding, playing-for-keeps exhibition. We see this in local games every Saturday from batsmen like Kenny, Bond, Knight, and others, and the performance by the visitor was not appreciated.' The other, surprisingly, was Chapman: 'We have been "fed up" with reports of his brilliancy in the field, and perhaps looked for too much. Undoubtedly his work was very sound, and he has an accurate underhand return to the wickets that quite fascinated the crowd, but beyond this fine asset he was very ordinary.' It seems, moreover, that the swell of criticism surrounding the tourists was at about this time gathering an extra dimension, to judge by a report from Wellington, entitled 'Mixed Cricket Teams', that the *Sun* also printed on Tuesday:

More and more, those interested are coming to the conclusion that if cricket teams of amateurs and professionals are to be brought to New Zealand, the distinctions observed in England must be dropped absolutely while the visitors are in this country, if the tour is to be carried out smoothly. New Zealand is a democratic country; at least, it always claims to be, and it certainly carries out its profession in anything to do with sport. Each time a mixed body of players comes to this country, stories of distinctions made within the team itself circulate and, whether true or not, they do harm. New Zealanders themselves are not prepared to treat an amateur better than a professional cricketer. If there be any way of avoiding it, they will take that course, and the sooner the point is realised the better for the prospect of tours.

No names, no pack-drill, but the broad implications were clear enough.

Meanwhile, as the criticism rumbled on, the MCC party was enjoying a mid-tour break from Tuesday to Friday: Swan stayed behind in Dunedin; Chapman and Lowry spent some days in the Geraldine district in South Canterbury as the guests of the Burdons, a big landowning family; five of the team went to Lumsden to get in some fishing; and the rest spent a couple of days in Queenstown by the southern lakes. The majority of the party then regrouped in Invercargill, the bottom of the world, for the two-day match against Southland beginning on Saturday the 20th. The Southland Pipe Band escorted the tourists from the railway station to the Grand Hotel, while at the Show-grounds the actual match was played to the strains of the Hibernian Band. These attractions notwithstanding, it was probably not the most popular bit of the tour, since Invercargill at this time was still a strictly 'dry' town. It was also almost a fatal stage for Freeman and Ferguson, who nearly ran off a steep hill into the sea when the brakes of a motor car they were in failed. As for the cricket itself, Southland, no great side anyway, were without one of their more promising young players, as the *Southland Times* had recorded a week or so earlier: 'Bogue has given up the game for the present. His decision is accounted for by the fact that to play here [i.e. in Invercargill] he has to undertake a sixty mile motor-bike ride every week, with the ever-present possibility of breakdowns on the way, in addition to lack of practice.' For their part, MCC introduced a new player in the form of Basil Hill-Wood, Wilfred's brother, who had come out to New Zealand on holiday. An occasional per-former for Derbyshire, he was a quickish bowler and could be effective, according to the *Cricketer* some years later, 'when he could get his late swing to work'.

The Showgrounds were in poor nick for the match: the wicket was bad, the outfield rough, and the grass long. About 2,000 watched on Saturday, but only 600 on Monday, as MCC won at a stroll by 196 runs. The best batting was Calthorpe's 77 on Saturday, with 'his freedom and brightness bringing frequent applause from the grandstand and especially from the ladies who mustered well in the front benches'. Southland made a reasonable 153 in the first innings, but, after Hartley had reversed his batting order and gone for an early declaration, could do nothing against Calthorpe on Monday afternoon. Basil Hill-Wood, with his fifth ball, took the final wicket. The *Southland Daily News* was less than happy about the local team's display:

The failure of batsmen who had been playing good club cricket can be ascribed only to nervousness and to a lack of realisation that the province expected them to uphold its honour and not to lash out at deliveries they could not possibly command in direction . . . . Southland cricket needs more vim put into it, and this energy will not be

'Our Party at Paradise'
Back row: *Tyldesley, Maclean, Unknown, Dorothy Calthorpe, Calthorpe, Gibson, Freeman, Titchmarsh, Swan*
Front row: *Wilson, Pope, Unknown*

displayed until batsmen are coached properly, bowlers are taught to cultivate length, and fieldsmen know that funk will not be tolerated. Men in the team for mere personal glory, men not prepared to take the hard knocks in the field, are little credit to themselves or to their province.

The same paper included an interesting description of the visitors in action:

The English bowling, and it is for the most part slow, is rendered effective by the close study the captain has made of his field. With Freeman and Tyldesley bowling, he plays three slips in sextant fashion and within touching distance of one another. The square-leg stands forward of the wicket and almost at a silly mid-on position . . . . Ordinary bowlers with such a cramping field must keep down runs against batsmen who show so little initiative as did the Southland eleven in the second innings. The backing-up system is almost perfect,

97

Invercargill

and bowlers at once resent fast stuff from the field, Calthorpe being particularly careful of his valuable hands.

Hartley himself, the master strategist, told the *Southland Times* that 'they always aim to have a man where catches are likely to go, even if it involves sacrificing a run or two'. He also 'expressed the hope that the visit would stimulate interest in the game in Southland', adding on a personal note: 'He knew that New Zealanders were very keen on rugby football, but one could not play rugger all the year round, and, having himself played other games, polo, rugger, and golf, he could say he got as much pleasure out of cricket as any other.'

Elsewhere, as the elegant Calthorpe charmed the ladies of

Invercargill, Kortlang was having a miserable Saturday for his
club, scoring 4 and 1 as Hutt (under McGirr's captaincy) won
by an innings and 59 runs; while on Monday, in the annual
match at Geraldine between old Christ's College boys and old
English Public School boys, Swan made another appearance at
the crease, notching a single before falling leg-before. During
the speeches at luncheon, he said that two other members of the
MCC party, Chapman and Lowry, 'would have been there, but
had begged off to attend the Wellington races'. That same day,
MacLaren, now back in Wellington from Christchurch, gave
another interview. He dwelt partly on the New Zealand team –
saying that whereas several of the batsmen would get into
English county elevens, McGirr was the only bowler of real
promise – but mostly on the recent press criticisms of the
tourists. 'He made no attempt to conceal his indignation at the
comment of the Christchurch *Sun*' and strongly supported
Hartley's captaincy on the final afternoon of the Second 'Test':

If the critics are angry that we did not sacrifice our best batsmen so
that we should lose possibly in an endeavour to do what any cricketer
regards as an impossibility, why do they not parcel out the share of
blame to the delay in starting the match when play did not commence
till two o'clock on the first day? I do not propose to criticise the
captaincy of Snedden, but he must have known, as we knew, that we
could not get the runs he set us, and that we were not going to throw
away our wickets. I asked this question in Christchurch and they said:
'We are afraid of Chapman if he gets going'. If they took the trouble to
observe the amount of work Chapman did in the field all day and the
distance he had to walk between overs from deep extra cover on one
side of the wicket to the same position on the other, they should know
that he was too tired to be expected to play a great innings. Then they
anathematised Wilson for scoring runs slowly. What am I to say to
them? They don't try to understand that Wilson is temporarily off his
game, nor that it is necessary to have in every side a man like him that
can play bowling for a long time and content himself with that, when
the needs of his side demand it. All the players of the English team are
doing their best, and many of them are very upset at the nature of the
criticism heaped on them in New Zealand. I tell them that it is
because of a very natural feeling of disappointment that New Zealand
has not defeated us, and, frankly, that the critics we have met are not

as cognisant of the fine points of cricket as they are in rugby, in which the voice of New Zealand critics is listened to with respect in every country.

He concluded by saying that he hoped to be fit to play in the Third 'Test', due to begin at Wellington on Friday week, February 2. These remarks off his chest, MacLaren on Tuesday attended the match at Kelburn Park between the junior representatives of Wellington and Canterbury: 'He followed the game closely, and at the conclusion spoke to the assembled teams, giving them some words of advice and congratulating them on their performance.' Over at the Basin, similarly encouraging words were perhaps coming from Kortlang, for during this week he acted as 'honorary coach' to the rest of the Wellington team as they prepared for their match with MCC starting on Friday. But before then, there was yet another mini-controversy. It seems that at some point after his return to Wellington, MacLaren, in front of a roomful of people in the Midland Hotel, made remarks to the effect that in the course of the Christmas match at Christchurch the wicket had been watered overnight in order to improve Canterbury's chances. Word reached Christchurch of MacLaren's remarks and now, on Thursday, the caretaker at Lancaster Park, H. Vagg, described the accusation as 'a downright lie'. By this time MacLaren had been joined by the rest of the team, which on Thursday evening attended a fight at the invitation of the Wellington Boxing Association. The following morning a statement appeared in the press:

Now that the MCC team has left the South Island, the management committee of the NZCC wishes to make an official statement regarding the tour to date. The necessity for this arises from the fact that certain articles have appeared in a section of the press which are unfair to our visitors, and have created a feeling of unpleasantness that members of the committee wish to dispel. The public has little idea of the difficulty of getting a side together in England to make this tour, and the difficulty is increased this season by reason of another MCC team being sent to South Africa. Throughout the negotiations, which extended over three years, the NZCC received every help and encouragement from the MCC, and at last every difficulty was overcome

100

and the team was sent. The extent of our obligation may be judged from the fact that the MCC voluntarily offered to bear half of any loss while we took all the profits. Unlike the Australian teams, the amateur members of this team receive no allowances, and each of them will be considerably out of pocket over the tour. Surely, under circumstances such as these, it is the duty of the New Zealand public and the press, which is supposed to express the opinion of that public, to extend every courtesy and consideration to our visitors. The management committee desires to express its thanks to the MCC for sending such a good team to the Dominion. It congratulates Mr MacLaren and the members of the team upon the very fine display of cricket they have given so far. It regrets that any unpleasantness has arisen, and begs those members of the team who had been offended to accept its apologies and its assurance that the unfair criticisms do in no way represent the feelings of those responsible for the management of the game, or the opinions of those best qualified to judge cricket.

'An Outing on the River'

·6·

The six that wasn't — Kortlang starts twitching —
telegrams and anger — Swan fails again — more chaff
for Hartley — Massey's finest hour — some like it hot
— MacLaren takes his leave — the boys follow

The match against Wellington was probably the best of the
New Zealand portion of the tour. Wellington's major problem of selection concerned the wicket-keeping position: with
Condliffe and Cate both unavailable, they decided to draft in
H.J. Tattersall, who had only very recently started playing for
the Midland club. Tattersall's career had been patchy in the
extreme: before the war he had played a couple of times for
Auckland and also gone to Australia in 1913-14 as reserve
wicket-keeper, playing only one first-class match there; while
since the war his sole representative appearance of any significance had been for Manawatu in a Hawke Cup match against
Poverty Bay in 1919-20. Not surprisingly, his selection aroused
a certain amount of local cricitism. Thirty six hours of continuous
rain put paid to Friday, but by Saturday morning the sun was
at last shining on a sodden Basin Reserve. MacLaren, 'still
limping', joined Hartley in the pre-match pitch inspection, but
in the event Collins won the toss and decided to bat, not
unreasonably reckoning that the sun would make the wicket
more difficult as the day went on. A crowd of three and a half
thousand was present to watch a hectic day's cricket.

Wellington batted poorly and were all out for 104 soon after lunch, by which time the wicket was perceptibly getting quite sticky and spiteful. Hiddleston top scored with 38, having given an easy caught and bowled chance early on to Gibson, while Wiri Baker in the middle of the order made a redoubtable 35. Kortlang was caught and bowled by Gibson for a duck and Collins, Bernau, McGirr, and Brice (run out) contributed but 11 between them. 'While Baker and Tattersall were at the wicket', the *Dominion* noted, 'the Englishmen in the field had some slight assistance from a fox terrier, whose anxiety for the fate of one of the batsmen reminded many of the dog Pincher, in the famous match at Piper's Flat, who bolted with the ball and thus helped McDougall top the score against Molongo.' After the last wicket fell, MacLaren was asked for his view of the Wellington batting and adjudged it a 'dreadfully disappointing performance'. When MCC went in at a quarter to three, they found that they had, according to Wilkinson, thirteen against them, 'eleven in flannels and two in white coats'. First out was Wilkinson, leg-before to Brice for 0. The recognised MCC batsmen found runs hard to come by, though Titchmarsh made 21 and Chapman 18. 'Calthorpe gave Kortlang a hard chance in making his first stroke, and two balls later he was clean bowled by Brice', for another of the day's ducks. He was followed by the crouching Hill-Wood, who 'brought a light comedy touch to the performance that kept the spectators simmering with enjoyment. He just let the ball find the bat, one of his strokes travelling along the turf but two feet from the blade.' Brice finally bowled him for 4. After tea MCC hit out, to get Wellington back in while the wicket was still bad, and a vigorous 29 by Maclean took them to a total of 107 in ninety minutes. The bowling star was Brice, who 'changed his usual style and tossed up slow stuff, turning both ways, with an occasional fast, straight one'. His figures were 5 for 52 and he 'was given three cheers as he came into the pavilion'. At the end of the innings MacLaren was again asked for his opinion and answered crisply, 'Difficult wicket'.

Wellington were left with about an hour and three-quarters to bat, so Collins rearranged his order in the hope of saving the main batsmen for Monday. It proved a vain plan, as the wickets continued to tumble. Hiddleston and Tattersall both batted soundly for 17 apiece, but Collins made only 2 and Kortlang was bowled by Gibson for 9. Bernau (19) and McGirr (7) tried to hit their way out of trouble: 'In running four for a forceful stroke, McGirr somersaulted in making sure of getting to the crease. That was the finish to his brief display, as he was stumped from the next ball.' Baker made a somewhat unfortunate duck: 'He touched a ball from Gibson, and it lodged somewhere about the wicket-keeper's body, where he could not get at it. Maclean huddled his body for the requisite five seconds, and when the umpire gave his decision a comrade seized the ball and flung it in the air.' The twenty ninth and last wicket to fall on Saturday was off the fifth ball of an over bowled by Calthorpe: 'It was not long before the time for drawing stumps when Brice took his place at the crease. However, he was deprived of a chance of batting. In attempting to run three for a stroke by Dempster, he was just too slow in getting to the crease. That was the end of the day's play.' So for the second time within a few hours Brice was run out for 0, leaving Wellington at 104 for 9, with the young Stewie Dempster on 16.

By the time that play resumed on Monday morning the total was down to 102, with Collins having accepted an appeal lodged by Hartley that a lofted straight drive by Bernau in Wellington's second innings had landed inside, not outside, the boundary rope. The game was still wide open, especially as rain on Sunday night was followed on Monday by a strong wind to dry the pitch. Dempster and Mat Henderson proceeded to bat sensibly for almost an hour, taking the score up to 133, at which point there was 'disclosed a leaf from the book of a master fieldsman': 'The ball was hit by Dempster slowly to cover, and he called to his partner to run. Chapman swooped down on the ball and threw the wicket down at the bowler's end in a flash, with Dempster a yard out. It was done in the twinkling of an eye and, as Chapman passed through the crowd on his way to the pavilion, he was heartily applauded for his brilliant piece of work.' MCC required 131 to win, but were quickly in deep trouble at 21 for 4, with Brice having clean bowled the notable quartet of Wilkinson for 1, Lowry for 3, Chapman for 5, and Calthorpe for 0. But Titchmarsh remained solid at the other end and eventually he found in Hill-Wood a partner of like-minded obstinacy. While the Hertfordshire stalwart 'gave a finished exhibition, placing his pull shots very nicely', Hill-Wood 'adopted curious methods in defence' and several times 'ran back almost on his wicket, following the ball till he got the bat in front of it'. Steadily through the afternoon the two of them took the score up to 108, when Titchmarsh was bowled behind his legs by Brice for 64 (refusing to go until the umpires had conferred) and four runs later Hill-Wood followed for 21, caught off Henderson. Maclean and Hartley then hit off the remaining runs, though not without incident, as the *Dominion* related: 'During Hartley's stay at the wickets he appealed to Collins to quieten Kortlang's movements: the fieldsman was standing close in at "silly" mid-off, and was moving here and there quickly in his anxiety to stop scoring strokes. The crowd murmured disapproval of the action of the English captain.' What really happened, according to Carman, was that Kortlang was making faces at Hartley. And that when Collins had a word with him, he replied: 'Every time I look at him [Hartley] and that little "mo" of his, it makes my face twitch.' Brice's figures in the second innings were 5 for 45. A crucial factor was the poor wicket-keeping of Tattersall, who, obeying instructions from Collins to stand back, still conceded 20 byes on Monday. But even with that handicap, Wellington had made MCC work hard for victory in what was, in Carman's apt words, 'an enthralling contest where every run was a bonus'.

That Monday evening, the 29th, the New Zealand team for the third and final 'Test', starting at Wellington on Friday, was announced to the press from the NZCC's headquarters in Christchurch. It revealed two changes: Cate for Condliffe and McBeath for Allcott. In the light of the recent match at the Basin, the Wellington critics the next day gave a thoroughly jaundiced response to the announcement. Thus 'Burwood' of the *Dominion* wanted to know why Brice had not been chosen, implied that this was assuredly not the fault of Tucker the Wellington selector, declared that Snedden was not worth his place as a batsman, certainly compared to Hiddleston, and concluded that being both player and selector put Snedden in 'an invidious position with the public and critics'. The *New Zealand Times* made the same point: 'A selector should not be an active player, and it is better if he is not connected with the management of cricketing affairs. Let him be aloof from everything of this nature, and then the black rumours of prejudice and favouritism will never be abroad.' The Wellington papers on Wednesday were full of letters complaining about the non-selection of Brice. 'Oh, for the sound of the voices when the Auckland captain-selector appears on the ground', wrote one enthusiast calling himself 'Justice'. The following day a letter appeared in the *Dominion* from Brice himself, criticising 'Justice' over his prediction of a hostile reception for Snedden on Friday: 'Nothing would be more degrading to cricket generally, and Wellington cricket in particular, and I sincerely trust nothing of the sort will happen.' By the time that Brice's letter was published, however, the whole situation had fundamentally changed, as a report from Auckland on Thursday made clear:

N.C.Snedden described today the methods of selection of the New Zealand side. The selectors decided to make the Third Test selection by correspondence, each of them making a provisional choice subject to review, as suggested by Mr Tucker, after the Wellington match, so that the Wellington bowlers' performances might be judged. Mr Snedden did not receive any communication from Mr Tucker after January 25. He did not hear the result of the match until late on the evening of last Monday [the 29th], and was surprised when the eleven was published the following morning. Before the Wellington – MCC match, the selection of Brice was a matter of doubt, but on his performance in that game he was regarded as a certainty. Mr Snedden forwarded the following telegram to Mr Tucker: 'Surprised your publishing team without reference to me. Consider Brice should replace McBeath. I have resigned selectorship. Will not play Third Test. Consider Wellington press attacks unjustified and prejudicial. My letter of January 26 agreed wait until Wellington bowlers' form in match could be seen.'

Reaction to this shock decision of Snedden's was divided: the Auckland press felt that Snedden, apparently not consulted, had been shabbily treated, but the Wellington lobby preferred to point out that certainly by Monday morning Snedden could have been reading in Auckland's newspapers about Brice's five wickets on Saturday. Anyway, with Snedden now out as a player as well as a selector, Tucker and Martin at this stage did the obvious thing, which was to replace Snedden with Brice and to keep McBeath in the side. The Wellingtonians had got their way, though Hiddleston was still in enough of a huff to decline to be twelfth man and so was replaced by Dempster. Finally, on February 12, a somewhat belated statement issued by the NZCC revealed the true cause of the whole charade:

The selectors, Messrs Snedden, Tucker, and Martin, arranged a tentative team, with agreement to reconsider the selection if occasion arose from the Wellington v MCC match. The instructions to the selectors were that the names chosen should be communicated to the Council on the evening of the 29th January, the last day of the Wellington match, so as to allow players to be brought from a distance. At 1.15 pm on the 29th ult, Mr Tucker sent a wire giving Brice's performances to Mr Snedden. He addressed the wire, 'Snedden, solicitor, Auckland'. That day being a holiday in Auckland, the telegram did not reach Mr Snedden, but was placed in the letter-box of another Snedden, also a solicitor in Auckland. Not receiving any reply, Mr Tucker concluded that the tentative team stood and, as arranged, he wired the selection to the secretary of the Council, who handed it to the Press Association the same evening.

To which one might add that the telegram might not even have reached Nessie Snedden on a working day, in that he had not just one, but two brothers living in Auckland who were also solicitors.

Most of the tourists were well away from the irascible controversy as it unfolded, making the briefest of return visits to South Island to play a two-day match at Nelson on Tuesday and Wednesday against a combined team representing the West Coast, Nelson, and Marlborough Associations. The *New Zealand Free Lance* related an episode that took place on the overnight steamer: 'A look at the bunks satisfied one of the side they would have a job to stow Swan's bulk away in one of them. The fellow swabbing the cabins looked at the English manager when the enquiry was made where they could put him away. Prefacing his remark with an expectoration on the floor, he was "darned if he knew". The disgust on Swan's face at the action and the remark was something to remember.' Swan in fact was part of a rather depleted team that took the field the next day: Basil Hill-Wood bowled 22 overs and took three wickets – one of which was a catch taken by a certain P.H. Slater, a tall man who, complete with cricket bag, had been following the team around at his own expense and was known to the cricketers as 'Pussyfoot'. After the combined team had been dismissed for 119, Wilkinson and Chapman made half centuries in MCC's reply of 249. Slater scored 1 and Swan rather less, but Basil Hill-Wood contributed 19. Nelson then collapsed for 55, Freeman taking 6 for 27. An exhibition display of batting followed to fill up Wednesday afternoon, highlighted by a towering six over the pavilion from Wilkinson. Looking back on the match a few days later, the *Nelson Evening Mail* reckoned that the wicket and outfield at Trafalgar Park had not been too bad and that 'if only the regular use of a horse machine and roller could be obtained, the ground would soon be in quite good order'.

Shortly after the tourists arrived back in Wellington on Thursday evening, news came through by cable from England that the old Lancashire and England batsman, J.T. Tyldesley, had died. For MacLaren, still unable to play because of his knee, it must have felt that the shadows were closing in. Still, there was a bright spot next morning, when the NZCC at Christchurch voted him an advance of fifty pounds 'against extra expenses incurred by him in connection with the tour'. For the 'Test' starting this Friday morning, there were no changes made from the MCC side that had played at Christchurch four weeks earlier, while for New Zealand, with Snedden absent, Collins was appointed captain. It promised to be a match full of runs, for according to the *Press*, 'the pitch was one of Napier soil, and Kortlang, who has had experience, said it was the nearest approach to the famous Bulli soil pitch [at Sydney] that he had seen'.

The *Evening Star* told the early story:

'Lucky' Collins won the toss, and with unbounded confidence opened with Blunt. It was misplaced confidence, however, and after cutting a single off Gibson, the captain poked Calthorpe's first ball into Chapman's hands at first slip. Gibson and Calthorpe were keeping a wonderful command of the ball and a beautiful length, while their variation of pace and spin [swing?] caused the batsmen no end of trouble. The pair raced neck and neck for an average, Gibson evening matters by getting Blunt caught behind the sticks, the unanimous appeal leaving no room for doubt. This left Shepherd and Dacre to carry on the good work. The pair were shaping comfortably, but did not combine too well, hesitating about sneaking singles. The Auckland colt, backing up over anxiously, called Shepherd wrongly. Clear and decisive came back the Dunedin veteran's command twice 'No, no'. But the boy was away, and in a wild scramble back had no earthly chance. The wickets fell: One for 1, two for 5, three for 19. It was magnificent, but it was not war.

From these early blows the innings never really recovered. Shepherd and Bernau played well, but on a fast wicket most of the batsmen were guilty of playing too much from the back foot. Brice, 'who was warmly received', made a patient 10 to help Bernau to add 57 for the eighth wicket, before, champing at the bit, he skied Gibson to Lowry at long-slip. The innings finally totalled 166 in 136 minutes, with Calthorpe taking 6 for 53. Titchmarsh and Wilson then batted in familiar vein, with the crowd of 2,900, especially those near the southern gate, being particularly hard on Wilson. When he was at last dismissed for 19 in eighty three minutes, 'the crowd made amends for its previous "barracking" by heartily applauding the outgoing batsman'. Soon afterwards, though, Chapman and Wilkinson were really brightening things up with a partnership of 103 in sixty four minutes, to take the score by stumps to 180 for 3. Behind the wickets, standing up to everything, 'Cate's exhibition was in marked contrast to the performance of recent "keepers"', though he still conceded 25 byes in the course of the innings.

After Chapman and Calthorpe had gone early – Calthorpe for the third successive time at the Basin bowled by Brice for 0 – Saturday turned into Lowry's day. He and Maclean put on 106 in an hour before Maclean was out for 53, after which Hartley 'was at the wickets forty one minutes for 16 runs and had to put up with plenty of chaff from the spectators', numbering some 5,000 on a very windy day. Lowry at the other end went on to score 130 in two and three-quarter hours: 'He got a great ovation as he returned to the pavilion, several of the crowd rushing to meet him and cheering lustily. Among those in the

On the road to Waikanae

stand who applauded more quietly was a pleasant faced lady.
She was the lad's mother, who had keenly watched the match
from its commencement. It was the first time she had seen her
son score a century.' The local correspondent of the *Sydney
Referee* described his style: 'Most of the runs in his century were

The Basin Reserve during the First and Third 'Tests'

made with shots on the on-side, 50 of them being made in a semi-circle drawn from square-leg to the bowler. The rising ball on the off he punches through the slips with a lot of pace.' MCC were all out for 401, no one emerging with great bowling figures. New Zealand again started poorly, but after tea Collins and

Blunt (dropped down the order) produced a good stand. Collins made most of his 69 while limping, having been badly hit on his leg by Gibson early on. The score at close of play was 178 for 5, with Blunt, following a disappointing series, not out for a determined 65.

Before the match was resumed on Monday, Ferguson published some figures showing rates of scoring for the tour up to and including Saturday's play. They revealed that MCC had scored in Australia at 62.69 runs per hour and in New Zealand at 89.02 rph; while the Australian states had scored at 79.97 and the various teams in New Zealand at 66.71. In the middle, the decisive wicket fell quickly:

Blunt had two warnings that disaster lurked not far away. There was a very confident appeal by the fieldsmen for leg-before to Gibson, but he got the benefit of the doubt. Soon after there was another and still more confident appeal for a catch at the wicket off the same bowler. Blunt admitted afterwards that he touched the ball. If Gibson had shouted down the wicket, 'Blunt, leave the off stuff alone', the warning could not have been more direct. But the batsman was determined to go for it, and it was only a matter of moments before he mistimed one, and the ball went into Freeman's hands in the slips.

Within the hour, obligatory flurry from Brice notwithstanding, New Zealand were all out for 215, Gibson having taken 5 for 65 and MCC winning by an innings and 20 runs. There followed an exhibition game for the hour before lunch, during which the tourists scored 87 for 5 and 'B. J. Kortlang acted as wicket-keeper for the New Zealand side and gave a good display, starting off by smartly stumping Wilkinson from the second ball.' But the match proper was over and with it the series. 'The result came as a great blow to all followers of the game, especially after the showing of the team in Christchurch and the brave fight made by Wellington', wrote the *New Zealand Times*. And it added: 'The bowling of the Englishmen was straight, good-length stuff, on or a bit outside the off stump, except when Freeman was bowling. Yet our batsmen kept sparring at it, or else trying to drive without throwing the left leg across the wicket.' The *Dominion*, looking back on the rubber as a whole, was bluntness itself: 'The play in each match demonstrated that New Zealand lacks temperament for big cricket and is not qualified to claim anything like international status.'

Early on Tuesday the tourists travelled to Palmerston North for their two-day match starting that afternoon against Mana-watu, Rangitikei, and Wairarapa Associations. The problems that the local cricket organisation had in trying to ensure a good crowd for a mid-week fixture were typical of the tour as a whole, with the four major associations having succeeded in reserving the more profitable week-end dates for themselves. It was probably a reasonable overall priority, financially speaking, but did rather mitigate against the proselytising aspect of the tour. In this instance, the Manawatu Cricket Association urged local business people to observe Tuesday as a half-holiday: a number agreed, but only on the condition that closing was universal; and since others refused, all the businesses in town stayed open. In fact about a thousand attended on Tuesday, which was not too bad granted that 'the boisterous high wind made conditions unpleasant'. They saw a curiously matched pair of openers: Freeman, who scored 3; and Calthorpe, freed from the cares of facing Brice, who scored 136 in better than even time. Hartley made 43 and at one point, according to the *Manawatu Evening Standard*, 'was apparently bowled, but he appealed for a rebound off the keeper's pads and it was allowed'. The next morning Hartley declared at the overnight score of 306 for 8 and, 'on a rapidly-drying wicket' (in the words of the local paper), the combined team were equally rapidly bowled out for 123 in front of a meagre crowd. MCC went in again after lunch, but soon declared at the mildly embarrassing score of 53 for 6, of which 36 were made by Willie Hill-Wood. A schoolboy called Bruce Massey, bowling with the wind and swinging the ball away from the bat, achieved the notable figures of 4 for 14 off 11 overs and was praised by Swan as the most promising bowler the team had encountered in New Zealand. Finally, the local team collapsed for 96, Hill-Wood and Wilkinson, the most occasional of bowlers, taking three wickets each. MacLaren was probably present at this low-key affair, but wherever he was, he would not have been best pleased to hear at about this time that Ponsford had just beaten his record score by making 429 for a Victorian eleven against Tasmania. Subsequent attempts by MacLaren to demote that match to second-class status failed.

From Palmerston North the team took the mail train to Napier, where they arrived on Thursday evening (the 8th) without MacLaren and Swan, who preferred to fit in a few extra days at the health resort of Rotorua. In addition, 'Hartley was away on a fishing expedition, while Lowry, Brand, and Freeman were on the sick list.' So once again, for the match on Friday

*'Well Caught': Chapman, Wilkinson, Lowry, S. A. Mannering,
Basil Hill-Wood*

and Saturday against Wairoa, Poverty Bay, and Hawke's Bay
Associations, it was Basil Hill-Wood and the mysterious Slater
to the breach. And indeed, after rain had delayed the start on
Friday, it was a useful 18 that Slater contributed to MCC's total
of 140. Chapman failed to score: 'Temperton's fourth ball beat
the newcomer, who thought he had been bowled and left the
crease. Ellis stumped him with promptitude and the batsman
retired.' But on Saturday morning, Gibson was altogether too
much for the local team, which, despite the presence of Bernau
(who had recently moved back to Hawke's Bay on business),
could manage only 68. In the second innings Bernau bowled
Chapman for 4, but an excellent 63 not out by Titchmarsh
enabled Calthorpe to declare at 163 for 4. Set 236 in a little
under two and a half hours, the combined team batted well
enough to save the game with some comfort. However, more
perhaps than anywhere else on the tour, the cricket in Napier
was not much more than an excuse for having a good time.
Quite apart from the lavish informal hospitality of the Lowry

family nearby, there were plenty of other attractions available during and then after the weekend, as the *Hawke's Bay Herald* itemised:

On Friday and Saturday nights the visitors were guests at cabaret dances in the Foresters' Hall. The lights of the room were subdued with red shades, giving a jazz effect, and Miss Healey's Jazz Band rendered excellent music from a dais which occupied the centre of the hall. On Saturday evening they were the guests of the Hawke's Bay Club at dinner, and early yesterday [Sunday] morning they enjoyed a highly successful kingfishing excursion in the bay, the weather being delightfully favourable and the catch a prolific one. They also visited Grassmere (Mr E. H. Williams' fine orchard) and other sights in the district.

The team and party, totalling eighteen, leave Napier per Aard specials at nine o'clock this morning. Mr E. H. Williams, President of the NZCC, accompanies the team. Luncheon will be put up by host Bishop and it is intended to picnic in the bush past Tarawera. The party will stop a night at Wairakei, and after a hurried view of the sights will journey on to Rotorua, reaching there Tuesday night.

On Wednesday the team played an *ad hoc* one-day exhibition game against Rotorua; the local team scored 110 for 6 declared and MCC in reply made 184 for 8, with Maclean, dropped frequently, scoring 62. They finally arrived in Auckland on Friday the 16th, with the return match there against the province having been put back from then to Saturday so that the tourists could have an extra day in Rotorua.

While the English party were picnicking in the bush, the NZCC met in Christchurch to consider a by now traditional theme:

Advance of fifty pounds to A. C. MacLaren. Mr Barrett reported that he had been requested to advise the management committee not to enquire too closely into the expenses charged by Mr MacLaren, and that at the conclusion of the tour the amount above that which the management committee considered reasonable would be refunded to the Council by the two gentlemen who had approached Mr Barrett. The chairman's statement was received, but the discussion following made it clear that in the opinion of the committee the guarantors would be called upon for a substantial sum.

117

Lunch on the way from Napier to Wairakei

Who these guarantors were is not known, but, to judge by an item in the *Weekly Press* later in the week, they would also have come in useful elsewhere: 'Amongst the accounts presented to the Wellington Cricket Association on Tuesday evening were the hotel bills for the members of the MCC team during their stay in Wellington. The item, "to pressing suit, 9s", appeared more than once. It was also evident that taxis had been used very freely between the ground and the various hotels at which the players had been stopping.' MacLaren himself decided not to stay for the final match in the Dominion. In the company of Swan and Wilkinson (whose period of leave was drawing to a close) he caught the boat from Auckland to Sydney on the 17th, but before he left he dispensed a last interview:

A New Zealand side, intelligently and carefully selected, would make a match with any of the English counties . . . . It is lack of proper coaching and consistent play with foreign teams, not Australian, that is retarding the advancement of the game. The practice of playing English touring sides, as in the case of the present team, against minor association teams, where in most cases 'bush cricket' prevails, is a farce . . . . Cricketers are to be discovered even in New Zealand. Brice, of the present-day cricketers, as a bowler knows more about cricket and its values than anyone else I know.

The general tone was kindly enough, if a little patronising, and the *Dominion* gave its account of the interview the rather touching headline, 'Salving the Wounds'.

The match against Auckland on Saturday and Monday was a dull, surprisingly one-sided encounter. Titchmarsh and Hill-Wood both batted well for half centuries, Calthorpe (78) 'indulged in an occasional "Harrow drive"', and Chapman scored a century of the highest quality. Allcott's figures of 6 for 86 compared well with Smith's 1 for 59. In reply to MCC's 365, Auckland were bowled out twice for 178 and 183, with Snedden, Smith, Dacre, and Garrard all registering ducks in one or other of the innings. McLeod hit well in the second innings until he was bowled by Brand for 50, the final wicket to fall in the New Zealand part of the tour. It was Freeman, though, who wreaked all the damage, with match figures of 12 for 158. From a playing point of view it was a most satisfactory *finale* for the visitors, but was soon overshadowed by the news that, on arrival in Sydney on Wednesday, MacLaren had started sounding off to the press in much sharper terms than had characterised his recent Auckland interview:

Mr MacLaren stated that the New Zealand tour was a financial failure. There were too many provincial matches, entailing much expenditure of time, energy, and money in travelling, which the gates seldom warranted. At Nelson, some of the New Zealand players hardly knew the handle from the blade of the bat . . . . He complained that a number of minor newspapers attacked his team and local players. These attacks he attributed to the ignorance of the writers, who, he said, were unacquainted with cricket. Mr MacLaren added that while in New Zealand, he rarely read reports of the matches, as they were not worth reading . . . . He did not want to play Freeman against the New Zealanders. The NZCC would not hear of it – they wanted the best team in the field. The result was that matches did not last until after lunch on the third day . . . . New Zealand batsmen were better than the bowlers. The latter had no idea of what was required of them in a tight corner. Their fielding was very weak. The men did not anticipate a stroke, but waited for the ball to come to them . . . .

119

The response in New Zealand was predictably indignant: 'The reference to the expenditure of time, energy, and money, which the gates did not warrant, seems especially ungracious. The team was supposed to be giving its time and energy for the good of the game, not for gates.' And the editorial in Thursday's *New Zealand Herald* continued: 'No one would expect Mr MacLaren to tell Australia that the general standard of cricket in New Zealand is high. It is too well known that it is not. To find him speaking in a sweepingly slighting tone of it, is to wonder just what is the cause and what the motive. What he has said is not tactful. Can it be suggested to Mr MacLaren, of all people, that it is "not cricket"?' The next day the vice-captain was at his diplomatic best: 'Colonel Hartley said he was not concerned. He did not believe the interview and never read interviews. There was no fly in the ointment as far as the tour was concerned, although a certain section of the press would have it so.' With those words, he and the rest of the team boarded the ship for Sydney. Perhaps Hartley's most tangible legacy to New Zealand cricket was a bat he had donated shortly before departure to the Auckland Cricket Association. According to the *Auckland Star*, it was to act 'as a trophy for the encouragement of cricket in the local public schools, with a suggestion that it go to the boy who "makes the highest score when runs are wanted"'. Such a bat, handle and all, would probably have got short shrift in Nelson, for from that town, on the same day (the 23rd) that the English team sailed out of New Zealand, there was sent to Auckland the most pointed of Press Association telegraphs:

Regarding Mr A.C.MacLaren's cabled comment on the Nelson match, Freeman, after the game, asked if it was the weakest team they had met, said, 'Not by a long chalk. You have some good cricketers. Saxon, who made 60, is a fine bat, as also is Kemnitz. Neale was unlucky, after appearing set, to be out for the best catch of the tour [caught and bowled by Tyldesley for 3]. Newman, with coaching, would be a first-class bowler.'

Mr H.D.Swan, the manager, as he was leaving, said: 'You have given us a fine time here; you have some good material'.

Mr MacLaren did not visit Nelson.

The **Free Lance**

An Illustrated Journal of Information and Racy Comment upon Topics of the Hour.

| 23RD YEAR OF ISSUE—No. 34. | WEDNESDAY, FEBRUARY 28, 1923. | EIGHTPENCE. |

Is It Cricket?
New Zealand Cricketer: "Archie the All Right! Why didn't you do this in
New Zealand, Mac, instead of waiting until you got to Australia?"

Rain in Dunedin — dew in Christchurch — Kortlang:
the facts — Shacklock solves mystery — MacLaren
still hors de combat — Liddicut's grubber —
MacLaren short of the ready — the balance-sheet
drawn up

While the MCC tour of New Zealand was going through its
final, rather leisurely motions, down south Wellington were
engaged in one of the more frustrating tours of the province's
history. After the fixture against Southland at Invercargill had
had to be abandoned because of rain, the caravan moved on to
Dunedin for the Otago match beginning on Saturday the 17th.
By Wednesday evening, after four days of nominal play, there
had been so much rain that the umpires declared the wicket
unfit and the match abandoned, with the scores standing at
Otago 331, Wellington 229 for 6. Kortlang had compiled a
painstaking 48 not out, but 'was hardly at his best as he was
unfortunately suffering from a recurrence of gas trouble con-
tracted at the war'. But irrespective of the umpires' action,
there could hardly have been a result in this match, since
the NZCC had ruled on Tuesday that, come what may, the
Wellington team were to leave Dunedin by Thursday evening
in order to be in Christchurch in time for the match against
Canterbury due to start on Friday morning. As it was, the
two-day match against South Canterbury at Temuka, due to be
played on Wednesday and Thursday, had to be deleted from

the Wellington itinerary. There was some dissatisfaction in Wellington about the NZCC's ruling, on the grounds that Plunket Shield matches were supposed to be played to a finish, but really the Council had no alternative: extending the Dunedin match would have fouled up arrangements in Christchurch; many of the players involved would have had difficulty getting further leave from their employers; and the cost involved – especially for the touring players, who received only the basic expenses – would have been substantial. In the unusual circumstances, Canterbury agreed that the winners of the Wellington match would take the Plunket Shield. It was a generous action, because the rules of the competition stated that the winner was the province with the most wins, Canterbury already had two wins to Wellington's one, and therefore she could still have lost to Wellington and taken the Shield by virtue of a larger excess of average runs per wicket for over average runs per wicket against. But a play-off it was, which gave a sharp edge to the next few days and indeed beyond.

Canterbury for this match enjoyed the services of Worker, even though he was now teaching at the Otago Boys' High School; while for Wellington, Brice and Bernau travelled down to South Island to strengthen the team. By the end of the second day's play, Saturday the 24th, the scores stood at Canterbury 225 and 10 for 1, Wellington 370. Wellington had taken almost six hours to score their runs: Hiddleston, 'as sound and stylish as ever, played masterly cricket' for his half century, but Kortlang's 53 in two hours was made, according to the *Press*, in 'a crouchy style that was far from impressive'. The *Evening Post* report stated that on Saturday 'the wicket showed decided signs of wear', so over the weekend the general expectation must have been that the Wellington bowlers would quickly wrap up the match. By the end of Monday, however, Canterbury's second innings score stood at 311 for 4, with Blunt and Patrick having put on an unbroken 153, a turn-about that prompted the *Press* to remark that 'the wicket played very well, and it is probable that Sunday night's rain had been just sufficient to bind and improve it'. The rest of the match had an inexorable quality to it: Canterbury on Tuesday took their score to 432 and Wellington in the final innings stood at 161 for 7 (Hiddleston

123

30, Kortlang 21); and on Wednesday, after rain had delayed play until 4.25, the last three wickets fell rapidly to give Canterbury victory and the Plunket Shield by 114 runs. Brice had performed manfully for Wellington, with overall figures of 10 for 174, but it had not been enough.

There was apparently more, however, to the match than met the eye, for on March 7, under the headline 'Do They "Play The Game" In Christchurch?', 'Touchline' of the *New Zealand Free Lance* made a serious allegation:

After breakfast on Sunday morning, two of the leading members of the Wellington team went down to Lancaster Park, and they found unmistakable evidence that the wicket had been watered after the cessation of play on Saturday night. On the actual wicket it was damp to the touch, and on the outskirts could be noticed the signs of where the water had trickled off, while seven yards at either end of the wicket they could not make the least impression on the turf by scratching with their boots. And, if this was not enough, the wicket had been rolled, and rolled well. No stated protest was made on the matter to the captain of the Canterbury team, but the matter was talked about amongst the players.

'Touchline' took the opportunity to quote the laws of cricket: 'The ground shall not be rolled, watered, covered, mown, or beaten during a match, except before the commencement of each innings and of each day's play, when, unless the in-side object, the ground shall be swept and rolled for not more than ten minutes.' Five days later the Lancaster Park Board of Control met and accepted Vagg's explanation that 'on the night referred to by the two Wellington players there had been a particularly heavy dew, and naturally it affected just the part of the grounds that had been most wetted prior to the commencement of the game, the wicket'. In Wellington, meanwhile, 'Touchline' had been having a chat with 'one of Canterbury's finest sportsmen' (Sims? Dan Reese?) and on the 14th he retracted his previous week's remarks, suggesting instead an alternative scenario that complemented Vagg's explanation:

The Canterbury plains are only thirteen feet above sea level, and in consequence when rain falls it only soaks a little way into the ground.

Christchurch is itself full of artesian wells, it being possible anywhere in the city to find water by boring even a few feet. Again, the dews there are very heavy, and the grass often has the appearance of rain for an hour or two after the sun has risen. This fact was pointed out to Mr A.C. MacLaren by Arthur Sims.

And 'Touchline' added that it was probably because of MacLaren's remarks about wicket-watering in Christchurch, circulating as they were around Wellington in late January, that the two Wellington players subsequently 'viewed that particular wicket with such distrust'. Honour apparently satisfied, Vagg now withdrew the legal action he had threatened to take against 'Touchline'.

The NZCC, meanwhile, had other residue of the season to attend to during March. On the 2nd, following 'the unanimous opinion of the members of the MCC team', it decided to award the prize for best groundsman to A. Ross, caretaker of the Carisbrook at Dunedin; and on the 12th, following a request by the Auckland Cricket Association, it met to consider whether Kortlang really had been eligible for the Plunket Shield match over Christmas. The crux was whether Kortlang in fact had arrived in New Zealand on June 19 the previous year, as C. G. Wilson stated on January 2, and had thus been resident for the necessary six months. Following an assiduous investigation by the management committee, it now turned out that Kortlang had arrived on the *Makura* at Auckland on July 7 and had therefore not been eligible for Wellington in December. Moreover, there was no evidence of Kortlang having previously played cricket in New Zealand except for the Vacuum Oil Company team in Wellington in 1921. The NZCC's statement went on:

From information collected, it appears that Mr Kortlang's cricket career is as follows: – He was born in Victoria and left for America as a youth. He played two seasons for the San Francisco County Club. In 1905 he played in Bermuda and for several seasons was a leading batsman in New York. He visited Australia in 1902, playing for the Balmain club in Sydney, and on a subsequent return from America played for the same club in 1908-9. 1909-10 he played for Victoria, and again in 1910-11 and 1911-12, also playing in the same season for

Middle Harbour, Sydney. In 1912-13 he again played for Victoria. Kortlang joined up with the Canadian Forces. After the war he again played in New York, and when leaving America in 1920 was referred to as having been a leading batsman during the previous few seasons.

These facts should show that the claim that Kortlang has been a New Zealand resident since 1910 is quite unfounded. The management committee, while replying to the question asked by Auckland, desires to give publicity to the facts, not with any feeling of hostility to Kortlang (who is in all ways quite desirable) but in answer to the criticism which has been levelled at the Council for refusing to play Kortlang in a Test match as a New Zealander.

Asked by the *Evening Post* for his response to this statement, Kortlang talked of the NZCC 'splitting straws' and 'doing its best to ruin the game', adding: 'Had I been playing in Canterbury – and they tried hard to get me to play down there – there would have been no question, in my opinion, whether I would be eligible.' At the end of the month he sailed out of Auckland on the *Maunganui*, bound for San Francisco.

Kortlang, though, was only a drop in the ocean compared with the problems the Lancaster Park wicket was to give the NZCC. Following a formal complaint being lodged by the Wellington Cricket Association at the end of March that the pitch had been tampered with – C. G. Wilson almost certainly to the fore in instigating this move – the Council agreed to the management committee holding a full-scale inquiry in Christchurch on May 8. Collins and Hiddleston attended in person, with the Wellington captain putting forward his prepared case:

When play ceased on Saturday, Mr Brice and he inspected the wicket. It was crumbled and loose on top, so that the ball could turn considerably. Henderson, at one end, had been making the ball rear in an alarming manner. The wicket was dry and dusty. On Sunday morning, about 11, Mr Hiddleston and he inspected the wicket. They found the wicket in a bad condition. They examined it carefully. Mr Hiddleston scratched a hole about an inch deep in front of the wicket, behind the popping crease. The earth was damp the whole way down. Mr Hiddleston went behind the wicket and found it dry and dusty – that was on a prepared portion of the wicket. They found all the bowlers' holes and those made by the batsmen very muddy in the bottom. One hole made by a bowler at the scoreboard end was not in the same condition as the others. It was dry and dusty.

Faced by questioning from R. B. Ward of the Canterbury Cricket Association, Collins then took a short one on the chin: 'When you found, as you say, that the wicket had been watered, why did you not protest to an official? – I was so damned angry. I lost my head.' Instead, Collins related, he and Hiddleston went back to the hotel, where he came across Blunt: 'He [Collins] said to him, "That wicket has been watered". Blunt said nothing, but put on his hat and walked out of the hotel'. Blunt's version to the inquiry was rather different: 'On the Sunday morning Mr Collins implied, in answer to a question as to how the wicket looked, that there had been something in the nature of a "local shower". He asked if Collins meant the wicket had been watered. Collins did not reply.' Hiddleston was also cross-questioned by Ward of Canterbury: 'Did you go down expecting to see a watered wicket? – I went down to see that it was dry. (Laughter).' And: 'What is your experience of dew? – I have never known it to settle on dust.' Also present at the inquiry was a clutch of local experts, together with Sims, who declared that 'if the wicket was watered, it was the dirtiest thing ever known in cricket in New Zealand'. Last word, though, went to Frank Shacklock, 'cricket professional of forty five years' standing', who 'said in his opinion the state of the wicket on the Sunday was caused by a heavy dew'.

Five days later the management committee published its conclusions and how it had reached them:

The full and free withdrawal of any suggestion of dishonesty on the part of Mr Vagg, or the members of the Canterbury team, narrowed the inquiry down to the two issues: (1) Was the condition of the wicket caused by the application of water by some person unknown? or (2) if not, by what means was it caused? There is no doubt in the minds of the members of the committee that Messrs Collins and Hiddleston gave an absolutely honest description of the condition of the wicket as viewed by them, and, without a knowledge of the local conditions, their conclusion that the wicket had been watered was a reasonable one. Having arrived at this conclusion, Mr Collins should have reported the position to Mr Vagg, who lives on the ground, or to some

127

official of the Canterbury Cricket Association, when the matter could have been investigated at once.

Rule 9 of the Laws of Cricket states that the wicket may only be swept and rolled between innings and for ten minutes before the beginning of the day's play. There is overwhelming evidence that this rule has not been generally observed in New Zealand. The custom has been to leave the time of rolling to the discretion of the groundsman. Mr Vagg's treatment of the wicket appears to have been quite impartial, as he rolled the wicket with a heavy roller early on the Saturday morning before Wellington batted, and, as worm casts appeared, again rolled it with a light roller immediately before play.

The evidence disclosed that it would be impossible for anyone without an intimate knowledge of the ground to have deliberately watered the wicket. The person doing so would require to know the locality of the water main in Lancaster Street, outside the Park, where the water is turned on; to turn it on he would require a peculiar iron key two feet long; he would then have to provide forty four yards of his own hose (for it is obvious that Vagg's hose was not used). Having surreptitiously done all these things, it would be necessary to provide a special fitting to attach the hose at the sump – the whole being accomplished in perfect secrecy. The committee cannot conceive that such a combination of unlikely circumstances is possible.

There then remains the contention that the condition of the wicket arose from the fact that Vagg rolled it with a heavy horse-roller while the ground was wet with heavy dew. The evidence of Mr Skey, the director of the Meteorological Observatory, shows that the night was one of unusual dew, or fog, and that the forming of mud on dusty ground was quite usual, and had been noted by him. The evidence of Messrs Sims, Du Feu [superintendent of the St Albans bowling green], and Marker [a bowler who had represented New Zealand] shows that a condition of great humidity on the grass in Christchurch is not unusual in the summer time, more particularly towards the end of summer.

The statement that the use of a heavy roller on dewy ground would cause moisture amounting to a small stream to be forced in front of the roller so as to cause the rivulets referred to by Messrs Collins and Hiddleston, appears to the committee to be quite a reasonable conclusion. On first consideration it would be expected that the hole behind the wicket would have the same appearance as those in front. Mr Shacklock suggests the theory that the moisture in front of the roller would be absorbed by the first holes, and that there would not be time to collect enough to affect the second. This appears to the committee to be a reasonable explanation, and the diagram drawn by Mr Collins at the time shows the holes to be in line, and supports this theory.

The fact that Messrs Du Feu and Marker, with their years of local experience, have made the same mistake as have Messrs Collins and Hiddleston shows both the practical certainty of the committee's judgement being right, and also the absolute honesty of the belief of Messrs Collins and Hiddleston.

The committee finds: 'That the condition of the wicket, as viewed by Messrs Collins and Hiddleston on the morning of Sunday, February 25, was caused by the groundsman rolling the wicket that morning, while the ground was wet with dew, and that such rolling was quite in accordance with local custom'.

Hiddleston, refusing to be blinded by science, was not convinced. Years later he was still describing it as the most peculiar dew he'd ever seen, being only in front of the wicket. And whenever a Canterbury sporting team arrived to play in Wellington, whether cricket or rugby, they would invariably be greeted from the quayside by a loud chorus of 'Who watered the wicket?' as they came down from the ferry.

* * * * * *

The final leg of the MCC tour involved four matches in Australia during March. There would have been five, but the week's delay caused by the shipping strike in December meant that there was no time for the proposed match in Brisbane against Queensland. While waiting for Hartley and the rest of the team to arrive, MacLaren in Sydney on February 24 wrote a letter of semi-apology to the NZCC, though it does not seem to have been received in Christchurch until March 15, whereupon it was published in the press:

In all my interviews I expressly asked the reporters to say nothing to hurt anyone, that there were some real good batsmen in New Zealand, that you were unlucky in finding two very fast wickets at Wellington most suited to our bowlers and batsmen, that we had met many real good sportsmen backing cricket, that the players themselves played good clean cricket, that a tour in England would give them the experience they wanted, and that I felt sure they would beat quite a fair number of the counties . . . . I will always remember you good fellows who did so much for us. If I can help your boys in England it will be with the greatest pleasure . . . . It has worried me a lot not to be able to take my place in the side since Wellington, and I am very sorry from your point of view that my knee has prevented my playing more. I have seen Sir Alan MacCormick here, and had X-ray photos of the knee. He said I should not play, as the fluid is sure to come on, any strain being put on the knee. I go to practice to see for myself, but find it is not too good.

MacLaren was still hobbling around with a walking stick when Hartley and his men made their taciturn arrival on Tuesday the 27th, as reported by the Sydney *Sun*:

'What kind of a trip did you have?' There was a giggle among all the team, lined along the railing of the *Ulimaroa*. 'You must see Lieutenant-Colonel Hartley. We can tell you nothing.' Not one, but all the members said the same thing, with the exception of Hartley, who had hidden himself and could not be found. But as the team dashed for the motor-cars outside, the vice-captain, Hartley, was grabbed, surrounded. He saw it was useless to protest. 'We had a splendid trip. There are some excellent batsmen in New Zealand . . . and that's all!' 'But what about the New Zealand press?' 'Look here! I never believe anything I read in the press – the New Zealand press. I cannot comment upon it. You know as much as I do.' 'What about the charges of extravagance that were levelled against your team?' 'Nothing in it! Nothing at all.' 'And the treatment of the professionals?' But by this time Hartley was in the car and, with a smile and a wave of his hand, had disappeared in the dust.

The match against New South Wales began on Friday and saw another creditable peformance by the tourists against the cream of Australian cricket. Titchmarsh early on missed a pull and was compiled to retire hurt, blood dripping from his face, but Chapman ('this giant with the boy's smiling face', as one paper called him), Brand, and Hartley himself helped to achieve a total of 275. On Saturday, in front of a crowd of 13,500, the local batsmen never got completely on top of Gibson and Freeman, though still totalled 314. Monday featured Calthorpe making a very solid 110 and Titchmarsh a plucky 36 out of a total of 296, though it is arguable that Hartley should have set New South Wales a more interesting target than 258 in eighty five minutes. Freeman again bowled well, but the match finished a tame draw.

The tourists then travelled to Melbourne, where they had easily the worst of a drawn two-day match against a Combined Universities eleven. Hill-Wood made a characteristic 84, but Titchmarsh, his confidence against quick bowling palpably shaken, was bowled for 2. There then followed, beginning on Friday the 9th, a remarkable match against a weakened Victoria team. On the first morning, the MCC batsmen 'showed little discretion in dealing with rising balls on the off' – MacLaren blamed the wicket – and were dismissed for a miserable 71. Titchmarsh was out for 1 and still needed seven more runs to complete his thousand for the tour in all official matches. Victoria then batted through to stumps on Saturday, with four centurions contributing to a total of 617 for 6 declared. Gibson and Freeman took 1 for 151 and 0 for 121 respectively. According to the Melbourne *Leader*, 'the Englishmen stuck to their heavy task well, but appeared to be extremely weak in the outfield. Chapman was head and shoulders above any of the team as a fieldsman.' On Monday, however, vengeance was presumably sweet as Hill-Wood and Wilson opened the second innings and proceeded to establish a world record by going right through the day undefeated. The final score was 282 for 0 and the match was drawn. Hill-Wood gave a difficult chance to slip and Wilson was twice missed behind, but in general they batted with great soundness, if painfully slowly for the first two or three hours. Liddicut in his frustration 'bowled one ball underarm, but it was a wide'. The *Argus* gave the highest praise to the batsmen: 'Australian soldiers learned from England how to dig themselves in on Gallipoli and in France, and here, on the Melbourne Cricket Ground, they saw two young Englishmen dig themselves in and hold their ground all day'. And apparently 'the spectators, who had begun by jeering, ended by cheering the stubborn Englishmen'.

The final match began at Adelaide on Thursday the 15th. With MacLaren and Swan following on, it was Hartley again who on arrival conveyed the official line to the waiting newsmen:

'A stop on the road'

132

'We have had a topping trip. There has not been a hitch anywhere. It has all been most enjoyable, and we are sorry it is nearly all over.' Earlier in the Australian season there had been talk of a coaching engagement for Harry Tyldesley at Adelaide, but it seems to have come to nothing. Moreover, it was at about this time that the news came through to the English party that the Tyldesley who had died had not been J.T., but instead J.D., one of Harry's brothers. Understandably, he did not play in the match against South Australia, though anyway he would hardly have enjoyed fielding out to a total of 495. Arthur Richardson played a symmetrical sort of innings: in the first over of the match he was dropped at point by Calthorpe off Gibson; at 140 he was dropped by Gibson off Calthorpe; and he was finally out for 280. Gibson again returned unhappy figures, but Freeman took 6 for 176. In MCC's reply of 372, there were good knocks by Calthorpe and Wilson, a duck for Titchmarsh, and a rapid 57 by Freeman that saved the follow-on. The rest of Saturday was a day of fiesta batting: South Australia scored 204 for 4 in 130 minutes, MCC 248 for 4 in 135 minutes, and the match was left drawn. Chapman rounded his tour off with a most brilliant 134 not out, including a massive six into the grandstand that struck a spectator in the chest. The only care-worn exception was the unlucky Titchmarsh, who, surviving one appeal, was then definitively leg-before for 5 and thus missed his millenium by two.

At the end of the match, Hartley on behalf of the rest of the team presented MacLaren with a pair of field glasses on the occasion of his silver wedding anniversary, which fell that day. MacLaren in turn presented Pope with a gold cigarette case. The next day Hartley and Gibson caught the train to Melbourne, Gibson bound for the Argentine and Hartley for some more fishing in New Zealand. And on Monday the 19th the others sailed from Adelaide on the *Ormonde*. Once the boat reached the Middle East, MacLaren despatched a typical cablegram to the Lancashire committee: 'Please post fifty pounds to Port Said to enable overland tour'. He received, however, the disappointing reply, 'Regret committee cannot accede to your request'. It is not clear what MacLaren then did, but he was certainly back in England by the end of April. The party as a whole disbanded in

Freddie and Dorothy Calthorpe on the Ormonde

the Mediterranean on April 18 and made their separate ways back home, Maclean for instance passing through Paris on the 19th and reaching London on the 20th. They had been away for almost seven months and it had perhaps been worth it.

* * * * * *

T. W. Reese, in his history of New Zealand cricket, pronounced a generally favourable verdict:

The tour aroused great interest, and although the Englishmen's cricket was not as a whole so spectacular as that of the Australians, it

134

was always good to watch. They won 11 games and lost none, but did not achieve this success without some hard-fought games. Otago and Wellington fought hard to the end, while the New Zealand match in Christchurch was drawn in favour of the home team.

Gibson proved himself a great bowler. Brand, the colt of the team, and Calthorpe were very useful all-rounders; but these three were the only ones who could much lighten the work of the two professionals. Tyldesley bowled a good slow ball, and Freeman's well-concealed googlies were perilous stuff throughout the tour. He always kept a wonderful length and commanded plenty of spin. Lowry hit in a jovial manner at times. Titchmarsh, Wilkinson, and Hartley were more circumspect, and had their reward in consistent success. The eyes of the whole Dominion, however, were drawn to young Chapman, who gave some thrilling exhibitions. He excelled in those shots which left-handers generally favour, the forceful cover-drive and the genuine square-leg hit. In the field he proved himself one of the greatest cover-points ever seen in the Dominion. Though MacLaren played only in four games, he taught New Zealand what had been the art which delighted Englishmen nearly thirty years before. Maclean, the wicket-keeper, always did well, and at times superlatively well, and proved himself a sound batsman.

Contemporary New Zealand opinion, however, especially in the protracted aftermath of MacLaren's Sydney remarks, was much less appreciative. Not untypical were the comments of 'Slip', cricket correspondent of the *Otago Daily Times*, on March 1:

That the Englishmen were too good for us was recognised early in the tour, but that does not get rid of the fact that they themselves are a second-rate team only, and not worth one-quarter of the amount which it cost to bring them out here as a stimulus to the game in our midst. As a matter of fact, the net gain so far as we are concerned is infinitessimally small, for the members of the side were so aloof that one could not possibly imagine for a single moment that they were at all concerned as to our welfare as cricketers.

Two days later the Napier *Daily Telegraph*'s 'Stump' took a similar line, stressing that the Australians two seasons previously had played much more attractive cricket and given much better value for money. And therefore, 'to improve cricket in New

Zealand, the governing body should not go beyond Australia to find teams to tour'. The question of value was forcibly pointed up some months later by the NZCC's annual report for 1922-23, recording in some detail the financial aspect of the MCC tour. Total expenses amounted to £9,379, of which £3,682 went on steamer fares (compared with £305 on steamer fares for the Australian 1920-21 tour). Of the more minor expenses, £59 2s 6d was the cost of MCC blazers and ribbons, while £6 18s 6d went to the 'massage account'. On the other side of the ledger, the money handed over to the NZCC from the matches played in Australia amounted to £1,587; while the gross receipts for the matches played in New Zealand were £5,862. The three 'Tests' produced chronologically diminishing gates of £937, £869, and £670. Otherwise, the best gate in New Zealand was the £756 for the Canterbury match. Bottom of the list was Nelson on £94, Invercargill on £142, Temuka on £160, and Palmerston North on £172. Taking the Australian and New Zealand figures together, gross income for the tour was £1,929 3s 6d less than total expenses; half of which loss was borne, as arranged, by the MCC. Yet the real failure of the tour was not financial, but rather, as 'Slip' suggested, social. Many years later, Eddie McLeod, without any sort of axe to grind, recalled how the English tourists had been 'a little bit off-hand . . . they didn't incline to mix with us'. And in this respect he compared them unfavourably with the Australians, relating how Mailey and Grimmett had once given Garrard and himself informal tuition in spin bowling. In the context of a fairly young team of whom only two members had been on a major tour before, much of the blame for this general failure in human relations must surely be attributed to MacLaren's rather detached, opportunistic view of the whole 'missionary' purpose of the venture. 'Skipper Archie MacLaren set out to enjoy *himself* on this trip. With that his main preoccupation, the tour inevitably suffered.' Ferguson's verdict is perhaps a shade harsh, but it has the germ of truth in it.

·8·

Old cricketers leave the crease — Lowry as leader —
Kortlang revisited — uphill all the way

MacLaren arrived back in England to find himself sacked as
Lancashire's coach, J. T. Tyldesley instead taking the position
at a much reduced salary. It also turned out that the First 'Test'
at Wellington had been his final first-class appearance, though
he did continue to play some minor cricket. During the years
that followed, MacLaren relied mainly on journalism to make a
living, though did try a variety of other wheezes on the side,
almost uniformly unsuccessful. His boat at last came home in
1939 when Maud inherited a substantial sum of money and
they moved into a sizeable mansion in Berkshire, where they
lived for the last five years of his life. MacLaren was seventy two
when he died of cancer in November 1944. He had outlived his
manager, Swan, who, after another ten or more years of happily
managing teams in his own relaxed style, especially MCC tours
to Yorkshire and the Channel Islands, died at Bournemouth in
1941 at the age of sixty two. The vice-captain, however, proved
a real stayer. Indeed, a few months after returning from New
Zealand, Hartley was off (under Wynyard's captaincy) on a
Free Foresters tour of Canada, where according to *Wisden* he
'bowled in his Oxford form of years ago'. After moving from his
home in Scotland, he finally died in 1963 at the age of eighty
eight at the Golf Hotel in Woodhall Spa, Lincolnshire. The

Horncastle and Woodhall Spa News noted in its obituary that Hartley had been 'very interested in local activities and supported the local Boy Scout Group and Darby and Joan Club'.

The 'colt' of the party had also played his last first-class match. Brand never did win a Blue and after leaving Cambridge he went into the City. During the war he served in Burma and was mentioned in despatches; in 1948 he became chairman of the English, Scottish, and Australian Bank Ltd; and in 1965 he succeeded his brother to become fifth Viscount Hampden. He died in 1975. One of the team's ringers, Basil Hill-Wood, played a certain amount more county cricket for Derbyshire, but, more interestingly, married Brand's sister, Joan, in 1925. Wilfred's days as a cricketer were also numbered: he had two excellent seasons for Derbyshire, but then virtually stopped playing for them apart from a few appearances in 1935 and 1936 when the county needed a captain. Instead, he too went into the City, becoming managing director of Morgan, Grenfell in 1939. He was a friend of George VI and continued subsequently to advise the royal family on their financial affairs. He died in 1980. Hill-Wood's partner on that famous day at Melbourne, Geoffrey Wilson, likewise had two more full seasons in county cricket, completing in 1924 a hat-trick of championship wins for Yorkshire under his captaincy, and then dropped out. In 1923 he was bottom of the Yorkshire batting averages, with 7.04 from 21 completed innings, and *Wisden* commented: 'With such a side at his command, he was not taxed as a captain, but it must be said that he seemed scarcely big enough for his position. Nothing that he did suggested any dominating personality.' Wilson then spent his working life as a director of the family business of Joshua Wilson and Sons, worsted coating manufacturers in Leeds. For many years he lived with his father (Gladstone Wilson) and mother in the family home at Chapeltown, but in 1954 retired to Southsea, where he died in 1960.

Titchmarsh, back on home soil, recovered his confidence and scored 781 runs for Hertfordshire in 1923 at an average of 60. He did, however, have the rather unnerving experience that season of playing for MCC versus West Indies and facing George John, who, though past his best, was still fast enough to pluck out Titchmarsh's off and leg stumps for 0, leaving the middle one standing. Over the next few seasons he continued to pile up the runs for his county and anyone else for whom he could fit in a game; but in 1928 his health broke down and, though he recovered to score 565 runs for Herts in 1929, he died in May 1930 at the home of his sisters in Royston, following a stroke that January. He was only forty nine years old. By contrast, two members of MacLaren's party were to survive into the 1980s. Wilkinson continued up to the war to play a good class of cricket whenever his military duties allowed him; and in the war itself (in which, 'for gallantry and distinction when in command of a battalion during the crossing of the Rapido river', he added a D.S.O. to his M.C. and G.M.) he played in Cairo against a Yorkshire Light Infantry team that included Hedley Verity, who got Wilkinson stumped. He died in 1983, still recalling iniquitous lbw decisions right to the end. The other long-surviving tourist, Maclean, played a full season for Worcestershire in 1923 and also represented the Gentlemen at the Oval, where, according to Warner, he 'kept wicket very well'. Early in 1924, however, he was one of the victims of the infamous Harris purge of those with suspect residential quali-fications. Kent lodged an objection, which was upheld by the MCC, that because Maclean's home at Ross-on-Wye was nearer to Gloucestershire than Worcestershire he was not qualified. Maclean's first-class career was thereafter more or less confined to playing for the MCC and the Free Foresters, though he did play three championship matches for Gloucestershire in 1930 and was even offered the captaincy. He later became Lord-Lieutenant of Herefordshire from 1960 to 1974 and of Hereford and Worcester from 1974 to 1976.

Gibson also slid back into a familiar routine in 1923, taking that year 65 wickets at 11 each for the Hurlingham club in Buenos Aires. The next year, following assiduous canvassing on his behalf by MacLaren, he was actually chosen, amidst much criticism, for the 1924-25 tour to Australia, but (quite possibly at his father's bidding) declared himself unavailable for business reasons. Granted the paucity of the attack that did go, it is just arguable that Sir Herbert cost England the Ashes. Gibson in fact only played two more seasons in England: in 1926 for Sussex, when he did relatively little, though twice bowling

Hobbs at the Oval; and in 1932 as captain of a visiting South American side. Following his death on the last day of 1976, a tribute in the *Review of the River Plate* summarised what he had done instead: 'For more than 30 years he presided over the fortunes of Liebig's Estancias [an enormous cattle-ranching firm] in Argentina, and throughout the Provinces of Entre Ríos and Corrientes, from highest provincial authority to humblest peon, the name of "Don Clemente" was a pass word which opened many doors.' And the tribute went on to describe how the 'administration of a big ranching' in those days involved 'interminable trips on hot and dusty trains, followed by back-breaking rides in a Ford A or even a modest sulky'. In short, Gibson 'epitomised the finest traditions of an old Scottish family who were great pioneers in Argentina'. He was also, though of course less importantly, one of the great lost bowlers of English cricket.

The two professionals who shared much of the bowling with Gibson in New Zealand had very different careers afterwards. Tyldesley, without MacLaren's support at Old Trafford, drifted increasingly into league cricket, playing for several clubs before he died at Morecambe in 1935 at the age of 42. Freeman went on to bowl for Kent up to 1936 and to take a total of 3,776 first-class wickets, including a record 304 in the 1928 season. But he only played for England twelve times, none of which was in a home Test against Australia. It is possible to take an apologia on his behalf too far – for the figures leave little doubt that in Australia he was not a particularly effective bowler – but at the same time there is surely something to the thesis (advanced by a recent biographer) that it was for somewhat suspect reasons that the selectors at home often preferred 'surprise' amateurs like Stevens and Peebles to the seasoned professional. The greater mystery about Freeman, though, is how it was that, with his *relatively* flat trajectory, he managed to get such an astonishingly high proportion of his victims stumped. Putting aside the spin element, which is obvious enough, a personal theory is that, with his rather low point of delivery and being a small man anyway, batsmen tended to estimate that the ball was going to reach a higher point in its flight (and thus went down the wicket) than in fact proved the case. But perhaps he took his secret with him to the grave in 1965.

Three of the MCC tourists later became Test captains. Calthorpe twice led an MCC team to the West Indies, in 1925-26 and 1929-30. The second tour was the more demanding, especially when Constantine started pitching it in short at the batsmen's bodies. Calthorpe at a banquet in Barbados criticised this bowling on both tactical and ethical grounds, causing a considerable local stir. In the final Test at Kingston, with the score standing at one each, West Indies had replied with 286 to England's 849 when Calthorpe confounded all expectations by deciding not to enforce the follow-on. It had been agreed that the match should be timeless, so he was presumably looking to set a four-figure target in the final innings. In fact, after England had scored 272 for 9 declared, West Indies stood at 408 for 5 at the end of the seventh day, whereupon it rained for two whole days. And, in what was to become one of the time-honoured ironies, the tourists then had to catch the boat home and the match was left drawn. Calthorpe himself relinquished the Warwickshire captaincy in 1930: he was, as the *Birmingham Post* put it, 'wearied of the tension of competitive cricket' and his bowling especially had suffered as a result. 'Not a very astute captain but always encouraging, particularly to the new and young players', was how Wyatt remembered him. Increasingly he turned to golf and to festival cricket, having been a founder of both the Cricketers' Golf Society and the Folkestone Festival. Fittingly, his last first-class match was at Folkestone, for MCC versus Kent in September 1935: Wilkinson opened the batting for MCC, while Calthorpe, batting at number ten, was stumped Levett bowled Freeman for 35 in the second innings. Two months later he collapsed on the fourth green at Worplesdon Golf Club, his home course, and died. He was forty three years old and had only just returned from a nursing home. Amongst those present at his funeral at Woking Crematorium were Swan, Chapman, and Major P.H.Slater.

Chapman ... The story of his life is such pure Scott Fitzgerald that it is tempting to quote the last (fragmented) words of *The Last Tycoon*: 'Action is Character'. By the time of his thirtieth birthday he had become England's captain for a decisive match against Australia that proved victorious, cap-

'Percy and David'

tained England to a 4-1 win in Australia, and been supplanted as England's captain almost solely because someone had to be the sacrificial victim in the face of the coming of Bradman. Certainly he had not developed into the major batsman that the early 1920s had presaged – his impetuosity saw to that – but he was still a talented hitter, an outstanding fieldsman (by now usually close to the bat), and by no means a bad captain. Perhaps it had all happened too quickly, for though he captained Kent from 1931 to 1936, he gradually became in the course of the next decade or so what has been graphically described as 'a musclebound alcoholic'. Becoming sales rep for a whiskey firm made the process irreversible. In 1925 he had married Beet Lowry, sister of Tom; they had met during May Week at Cambridge in 1921 and the romance was nurtured while Chapman toured New Zealand. They became close friends of the Calthorpes and also lived in Worplesdon. The marriage was dissolved in 1942. Chapman lived for the last fourteen years of his life in the home belonging to a golf club steward and died in hospital at Alton, Hampshire, in September 1961 after a fall in his bedroom had necessitated an operation on a fractured knee. He was by the end the skeleton in the cupboard of English cricket history, perhaps because he was everyone's guilty conscience.

His brother-in-law enjoyed a life of quite different fortunes. Lowry returned to Cambridge in 1923 and soon scored 161 against Lancashire. One of the umpires was Board and, according to the *Athletic News*, 'his delight at the success of his former pupil was worth going far to see'. Lowry finally won his Blue and the following year captained Cambridge to victory, while continuing to play for Somerset. He returned to New Zealand in 1925 and began farming in Hawke's Bay, but was persuaded by Wellington to captain the province, which he did for six seasons from 1926-27. During this time he also led the first two New Zealand tours of England, in 1927 and 1931, as well as captaining New Zealand at home to A. H. H. Gilligan's tourists in 1929-30. *Wisden* recalled him in his obituary as 'an outstanding captain', who 'aimed at winning, not drawing, insisted on absolute punctuality and abhorred waste of time'. While according to Carman, he was 'a great captain, more by force of

143

character than by persuasion'. Dan Reese described him as a captain who was 'always "chasing" the batsman' and who 'drove rather than led his side'; though both he and T. W. Reese felt that Lowry rather over-did the quick-change bowling tactics. There can be no doubt that as a captain he had precisely the sort of presence and character that New Zealand cricket, entering a new and testing phase, needed at that time. 'A quiet-spoken individual who could swear like a trooper if it suited him, but very easy to get along with', was Ferguson's characterisation of him as a touring captain. An interview in the Christchurch *Press* in November 1982 with the old Canterbury quick bowler Bill Cunningham suggested that Lowry on the 1927 tour failed to give Cunningham a fair crack of the whip because he objected to him on social grounds and his involvement in trades unionism. According to Cunningham, Lowry at Lord's even tried to prevent him meeting George V. It is quite impossible to know how much (if any) weight to put on such stories, but it is worth noting that, ten years afterwards, Dacre recalled that in 1927 Cunningham's length and line got so bad that 'one could not bat in the nets against him'. The controversies of captaincy apart, one of the most notable attributes of Lowry in these years was the increasing dependability he showed as a batsman, especially in difficult situations. He could still hit, but he now knew how to defend. Above all he loved a challenge, as Canterbury's Ian Cromb later recalled of the 1931 tour:

Against Middlesex we lost four wickets quickly and I was preparing to go into bat. Tom brushed me aside and went out to do battle against Gubby Allen, whom he regarded with a certain degree of disdain. In his hurry to get to the crease, Tom had forgotten to wear a box, and the first ball hit him where his protector should have been. In anger he threw his gear on to the ground and rushed off past the startled old gentlemen in the Long Room and put on a large wicket-keeper's box. The next ball he received from Allen he played with his stomach, just like a tank, to the amusement of all those at Lord's.

Lowry came to England again in 1937 as manager, though also played in quite a few of the county matches. On his father's death in 1944, he took over Okawa Station, which until his own death in 1976 he continued to run as both a sheep and cattle station on an enormous scale and also a prolifically successful thoroughbred stud.

Lowry's old school colleague, Blunt, proved one of the most reliable performers in both 1927 and 1931, as a revitalised leg-break bowler as well as a batsman. Blunt transferred in 1926 from Canterbury to Otago and in 1931-32, his last season in New Zealand cricket, he scored a superb 338 not out at Lancaster Park against his old province. At Lord's in 1931 he made an eminently watchful 96 against England, perhaps as fine an achievement. For the rest of the decade, most of his cricket was played on behalf of Sir Julien Cahn, who gave him a business appointment in Nottingham. He settled in England, became in later years the first captain of the London New Zealand C.C., and died in London in 1966. His one-time opening partner for Canterbury, Worker, put in a brief stint for Otago before he took up in the mid-1920s a teaching position in Napier, which enabled him to play for Wellington and thereby, in T. W. Reese's words, 'complete his circuit of the major provinces'. Further down South Island, three of the more prominent Otago cricketers of 1922-23 had varying careers afterwards: Galland never did make the New Zealand eleven, but he continued playing for his province up to 1931, even becoming 'a wicket-keeper of merit' (Carman) from 1927; Shepherd was selected for the tour of England in 1927, but on financial grounds felt himself unable to go; while Dickinson enjoyed a surprisingly long career for a fast bowler, his arm ever lower, but the unreliable streak that was always in him was further accentuated when he became a commercial traveller in the thirties.

Collins continued playing regularly for Wellington up to almost the end of the 1920s, as did Brice. 'Sixer' played several more years after that for Petone, into his mid-fifties, and finished with a grand total of 1,173 wickets in Wellington club cricket. After retiring from the Great Meat Co, he farmed for a while and also ran a hotel, before he died in 1959 at the age of seventy eight. Brice's natural successor, McGirr, went on captaining Hutt (who had won the Wellington senior league in 1922-23), improved as a batsman by steadying himself down a little, and in 1927 went to England, where at the Oval he had Hobbs caught for a duck off a rank long hop. He ran a sports shop in

Wellington, swearing by Nottingham nails in the boots he sold, and only gave up club cricket when, the day after scoring 70 at the age of sixty seven, he suffered a fall as he was taking in the milk at home. Also from the Wellington team on that 1927 tour of England were Bernau, who achieved little, and Dempster, who was emerging as *the* New Zealand batsman of his generation. In the thirties Dempster lived in England, where he played for Leicestershire and also for Cahn, to play for whom attracted him (unlike Blunt) more perhaps for the hospitality on offer than the actual cricket. Another potential prodigy of the early twenties did not, however, make it into the big time: the historian of schoolboy cricket in Palmerston North records how when Massey left school and moved to Wellington, 'he was induced, on the advice of the experts there, to bowl into the wind, coming in from the off', with the result that 'in the effort to keep them up his delivery became lower, and although he turned out a fine all-rounder, he never again bowled so effectively' – as, in other words, on that dream-like February afternoon when he sent back Wilkinson, Tyldesley (a great name), Wilson, and Hill-Wood.

Hiddleston, following his rather chequered season in 1922-23, then entered into his real prime as a dominant opening batsman. Twice over the next few years his season's aggregate exceeded 500 runs; and in 1926, with 103 in 110 minutes against Canterbury at the Basin, he became the first New Zealand batsman to score a century before lunch. In 1924 he was one of a touring party that visited Fiji (there is a marvellous long-range photo of Hiddleston batting in Snow's book on Fijian cricket), but he was unable to tour either Australia in 1925-26 or England in 1927. T. W. Reese later wrote: 'Good judges of the game are of the opinion that, had Hiddleston been able to accompany the 1927 team to England, he would have impressed the critics even more than Dempster did, for at that time he was the best batsman in the Dominion.' The reason given for Hiddleston's unavailability was 'business commitments', but the fairly reliable story goes that Hiddleston did in fact want to go to England and only failed to do so because the authorities in Christchurch took such a long time before they offered a definite place to him. Not that considerations of 'business' would have been negligible:

having been buyer for the clothing department of Sargood, Son, and Ewen's Wellington branch, Hiddleston in the course of the 1920s went into business as an importer on his own account. According to the *Evening Post*, 'as a manufacturers' representative he had many important interests' and 'was connected with numerous Yorkshire concerns, as well as others in England and on the Continent, dealing mostly in woollen and silk piece goods'. By the early 1930s he was no longer playing for the province, but still for a while turned out in club cricket. He died in 1940 at the age of forty nine, having gone into hospital for a non-essential hernia operation. His early mentor, 'Father' Wilson, lived for another twelve years and died in Victoria, from whence he had come, at the age of eighty four.

What of Kortlang? The *Cricketer* in May 1923 did its best to keep the cricket community up-to-date: 'He is now said to be on a tour of the world, with London and Paris in his itinerary, to arrange for the visit of a crack American baseball team to Australia, New Zealand, Japan, Hawaii, and the Philippines.' But later in the year he was back in Wellington, for whom over the next four New Zealand summers he played regularly in the Plunket Shield, amassing in all for the province (including the 1922-23 season) 1,293 runs at an average of 49. His highest score was a chanceless 214 not out versus Auckland in 1925-26; and in 1923-24 he was even permitted to represent New Zealand against the visiting New South Wales team. According to Brittenden, he 'taught New Zealand the hook stroke' and was also an important beneficial influence on the young Dempster. T. W. Reese, however, blamed Kortlang for inculcating Wellington's batsmen with his own rather dour, 'safety first' principles, which made the province, though successful, something of a trial to watch. As a figure in Wellington cricket during the mid-1920s, Kortlang remained a mystery: at the end of each season he departed for unknown shores, but invariably he would be back the following spring. It seems pretty clear that, in addition to his baseball-related entrepreneurial activities, he was some sort of commercial traveller, moving around New Zealand during the summer and elsewhere in the winter. And according to Jack Gregg, the products that he sold were Fluenzol, a coloured-water cough mixture, and Q-Tol, a thick, pinkish-coloured skin lotion, both of which blessings to humanity were manufactured in Australia. And indeed, at some point after he had retired from the cricket field, he moved more or less permanently to Perth in Western Australia, where he became known as the father of baseball there. It was from Perth that in 1959 he sent a letter to Carman that that year's *Cricket Almanack of New Zealand* summarised:

He said his real name is Harry Herbert Lorenz Kortlang, and that he was born at Carlton, Victoria, on 12 March 1880 [as opposed to the date that was usually given of 13 March 1883]. He said the reason he is known as 'B.J.' was that on his first appearance, the scorer did not know the initials but had heard him being called 'Bert' and 'Jack' by different people, so gave him the initials B.J. Those who knew Kortlang personally will appreciate that he wouldn't have worried what he was called.

The wanderings finally ended on 15 February 1961, the last day of the Australia – West Indies series, when Kortlang died suddenly at Cottesloe, in Perth, while he was out fishing. In manner of death, if not in life, he was at one with Hartley.

Another of Kortlang's old sparring partners, Nesbit Snedden, was soon back in the fold as a New Zealand selector after the *contretemps* of 1923. He went on playing for Auckland up to 1928 and for the Ponsonby club for a further nine years. His son, Colin, and great-nephew, Martin, later played for New Zealand. Smith also continued for Ponsonby into the 1930s, though stopped for Auckland in 1926, having averaged 41 with the bat and taken 140 wickets at 21 apiece. Perhaps surprisingly, after his experience in MacLaren's match, he was twice selected in 1923-24 for New Zealand against New South Wales. Smith died in 1963, Snedden in 1968. Auckland's other main left-arm bowler, Allcott, twice went to England (in 1931 as player-treasurer) and had his moments, including 5 for 3 against Somerset in 1927, but by this time was coming to rely as much on his batting as his bowling for a place in the New Zealand side. Thus six full Tests brought him only six wickets, at an average of 90.16. From the early 1930s, his job in the bank involved him in a peripatetic existence, and in the course of the decade he played minor matches for Wellington and South

Canterbury. Finally, in December 1945, he represented Otago against Auckland at Dunedin in the Plunket Shield, scoring 19 and taking 3 for 91 in the match. Of the other Auckland players, McLeod moved to Wellington in 1926 and played there in 1929-30 for New Zealand against England, scoring 16 and 2 not out; while Garrard went on playing for the province until 1942. By then, the boy wonder, Ces Dacre, was a name from the past, having decided at the end of the 1927 tour to try to establish himself in English cricket. So, 'entirely on his own initiative', to quote *Wisden*, 'he stayed behind to qualify for Gloucestershire, with whom he had family links'; and from 1930 to 1936 he was 'a valuable member of the side, without ever making quite the number of runs hoped for'. He played many brilliant innings, but never overcame his failing of being a poor starter. In the end, muscular rheumatism brought his career to a relatively early close. He died in 1975, with little interest apparently, in his later years, in what was going on around him.

Individual destinies, though, tell us only a certain amount about the collective fate of New Zealand cricket. The tour to England in 1927, which Swan played an active part in arranging, was of course a great landmark, for all its being one big financial headache from beginning to end. Of the twenty six first-class matches played, seven were won and five lost. The batting proved much stronger than the bowling (an old story that was not to change for a long time) and Titchmarsh enjoyed himself to the tune of 171 and 71 for the MCC at Lord's; while drafted in to open for the tourists versus the Civil Service at Chiswick (and soon caught for 4) was none other than an elderly Ronny Fox. Two years later, in 1929-30, Gilligan's men beat New Zealand only 1-0 over the course of four matches that were subsequently designated official Tests. At Christchurch, Lowry found himself being roundly barracked for wearing a blue cap rather than a New Zealand one, though in fact it was not his Cambridge cap, but that of his local club, Mowhoango. Significantly, Maurice Allom, in his account of the tour, noted how, on the team's arrival at Wellington, Dan Reese on behalf of the NZCC 'told us how much New Zealand appreciated the fact that England had seen fit to send out so very representative a side with its quota of professionals increased from two to six'. At the actual time, however, the first real Test that New Zealand played was at Lord's in 1931, when Lowry's team performed so creditably in a drawn contest that two more Tests – one comprehensively lost, the other virtually washed out – were quickly organised. 'Really a team of average county class plus a charm of demeanour not at all common in our counties' was the verdict expressed by Cardus in the *Manchester Guardian*, with which opinion most critics of the day would have agreed.

Yet after this relatively encouraging beginning, progress in international cricket over the succeeding decades was to be painfully and discouragingly slow. During the rest of the thirties (and arguably beyond) the indifferent attitude of the Australian Board of Control, seemingly mirrored by that of Bradman, did not help; while both before and to some extent after the war, the old problems of distance, lack of money, and lack of leisure remained formidable. Until recently, tours of England took place only at long intervals: 1937, 1949, 1958, 1965. And when England came to New Zealand for the ritual two Tests at the end of a gruelling Australian tour, the absence of enthusiasm on the part of the visitors was often only barely disguised. But a year after enduring the all-time nadir of being scuttled out for 26 by England at Eden Park, with Bert Sutcliffe the only batsman to reach double figures, New Zealand in 1955-56 on the same ground won her first Test by defeating the West Indies by 190 runs: Alf Valentine pushed forward to Harry Cave, was smartly stumped down the leg-side by Simpson Guillen, and within minutes John Reid, a life-long teetotaller, was toasting victory in front of an excited crowd. More heartaches and beatings of the breast then inevitably followed, but in 1974 the whole country enjoyed the sweetness of vanquishing Australia at Lancaster Park. And four years later at the Basin Reserve, over half a century after MacLaren had flayed the bowling at will, an England team under the captaincy of another famous opening batsman finally succumbed. Needing 137 to win, Geoff Boycott was soon yorked for 1 by Richard Collinge, who with Richard Hadlee then swept through the rest of the batting for an ignominious total of 64. Old ghosts and accumulated inferiority complexes had at last been laid to rest: the Cinderella of world cricket was now ready for the ball.

──·TOUR RESULTS·──

WESTERN AUSTRALIA v MCC

Played at PERTH   November 3, 4

MCC

Mr C. H. Titchmarsh lbw, b Lanigan	4 —	not out 50
Mr W. W. Hill-Wood c Fley b Buttsworth ..	13 —	c Fley b Buttsworth 6
Mr A. C. Wilkinson c Blundell b		
Buttsworth	40 —	c Howard b Buttsworth 0
Mr A. P. F. Chapman run out	75 —	c Blundell b Evans 58
Hon. D. F. Brand c Evans b Fley	21 —	not out 13
Mr T. C. Lowry c Carlson b Buttsworth ...	20	
H. Tyldesley c Buttsworth b Evans	0	
Col. J. C. Hartley b Fley	3	
Mr C. H. Gibson not out	4	
A. P. Freeman b Bott	6	
Mr H. D. Swan b Bott	0	
B 2, l-b 2	4	B 2, l-b 3 5
	190	**132**

WESTERN AUSTRALIA

C. Howard b Freeman	24	C. Fley c Chapman b Gibson 4
R. Blundell c Wilkinson b Gibson ...	10	J. Buttsworth c Titchmarsh b
V. Carlson b Freeman	4	Gibson 12
A. Heindricks not out	91	W. Stokes c Gibson b Freeman 5
L. C. Bott b Freeman	8	J. Lanigan st Lowry b Brand 11
A. Evans b Gibson	53	B 5, l-b 4 9
A. Meek run out	3	**234**

BOWLING
WESTERN AUSTRALIA

	Overs	Mdns	Runs	Wkts	Overs	Mdns	Runs	Wkts
Buttsworth	17	3	45	3	10	0	29	2
Lanigan	15	1	60	1	8	3	20	0
Meek	11	1	29	0	5	1	14	0
Evans	15	3	39	1	9	1	31	1
Fley	6	2	10	2	3	0	26	0
Bott	3.4	1	3	2	3	2	2	0
Carlson	—	—	—	—	3	0	5	0

MCC

	Overs	Mdns	Runs	Wkts
Gibson	38	11	68	4
Freeman	38	13	101	4
Brand	9.3	2	22	1
Hill-Wood	2	0	6	0
Tyldesley	9	0	28	0

Match drawn

Played at ADELAIDE   **November 10, 11, 13**

SOUTH AUSTRALIA

A. Richardson c Wilkinson b Tyldesley	150	— b Freeman	15
V. Richardson c Tyldesley b Calthorpe	118	— lbw, b Freeman	0
J. T. Murray c Chapman b Freeman	48	— c Chapman b Freeman	28
C. Dolling c Lowry b Tyldesley	24	— c Tyldesley b Freeman	0
E. A. Loveridge run out	29		
R. J. B. Townsend c Calthorpe b Freeman	18	— not out	10
A. G. Rymell c Freeman b Tyldesley	23	— not out	1
C. D. Gray lbw, b Tyldesley	16		
N. L. Williams c Calthorpe b Tyldesley	5		
R. Bennett b Freeman	5		
F. L. Martin not out	0		
B 2, l-b 4	6	B 3, l-b 3	6
	442		**60**

MCC

Mr W. W. Hill-Wood c Bennett b A. Richardson	15	— lbw, b Townsend	30
Mr A. C. Wilkinson c Bennett b Williams	64	— b Gray	6
Mr C. H. Titchmarsh run out	9	— b A. Richardson	41
Hon. F. S. G. Calthorpe c and b Loveridge	0	— c and b A. Richardson	17
Mr A. P. F. Chapman c Bennett b Townsend	32	— c Bennett b Townsend	53
Mr G. Wilson b A. Richardson	38	— b Townsend	61
Mr A. C. MacLaren c and b Townsend	12	— st Bennett b Williams	41
Mr T. C. Lowry st Bennett b Williams	1	— b A. Richardson	20
Mr C. H. Gibson lbw, b A. Richardson	17	— lbw, b Williams	3
H. Tyldesley c Dolling b Gray	6	— lbw, b Williams	7
A. P. Freeman not out	0	— not out	3
B 6, l-b 4, w 1	11	B 7, l-b 4, w 1	12
	205		**294**

BOWLING
MCC

	Overs	Mdns	Runs	Wkts	Overs	Mdns	Runs	Wkts
Gibson	10	0	53	0				
Calthorpe	11	1	75	1				
Freeman	27	0	169	3	2	0	23	4
Tyldesley	24	3	100	5	2.5	0	31	0
Chapman	2	0	15	0				
Hill-Wood	1	0	24	0				

SOUTH AUSTRALIA

	Overs	Mdns	Runs	Wkts	Overs	Mdns	Runs	Wkts
Morton	13	0	51	0	8	2	27	0
Townsend	13	2	35	2	15	0	75	3
A. Richardson	16.4	4	40	3	16	4	37	3
Murray	2	1	1	0	5	0	14	0
Williams	11	1	44	2	9.5	0	62	3
Loveridge	2	0	20	1	10	1	37	0
Gray	1	0	3	1	13	2	30	1

Lost by six wickets

Played at MELBOURNE   November 17, 18, 20

MCC

Mr G. Wilson b Wallace	9	— c Mayne b Hartkopf	3
Mr C. H. Titchmarsh c Willis b Wallace	11	— c and b Hartkopf	82
Mr A. C. Wilkinson c Hartkopf b Keating	62	— c Willis b Hartkopf	20
Hon. F. S. G. Calthorpe c Mayne b Wallace	10	— b Grimmett	19
Mr A. P. F. Chapman st Ellis b Hartkopf	73	— c Willis b Hartkopf	69
Hon. D. F. Brand c Mayne b Hartkopf	17	— b Liddicut	1
Mr A. C. MacLaren c Ellis b Grimmett	5	— c Mayne b Hartkopf	0
Mr C. H. Gibson b Hartkopf	2	— c and b Hartkopf	11
Mr J. F. Maclean not out	11	— c Wallace b Hartkopf	8
H. Tyldesley st Ellis b Hartkopf	4	— b Hartkopf	3
A. P. Freeman c Ransford b Hartkopf	0	— not out	6
B 3, w 3	6	B 4, l-b 4, w 1	9
	210		**231**

VICTORIA

E. R. Mayne lbw, b Gibson	17	— c Maclean b Gibson	15
R. L. Park b Freeman	11	— b Tyldesley	11
C. B. Willis c MacLaren b Gibson	5	— b Calthorpe	60
W. M. Woodfull run out	74	— not out	4
J. L. Ellis c Calthorpe b Gibson	0	— b Tyldesley	16
A. E. Liddicut run out	0	— c Chapman b Calthorpe	1
A. E. V. Hartkopf c and b Freeman	86	— not out	14
V. S. Ransford c MacLaren b Brand	26	— b Calthorpe	15
L. Keating c Chapman b Brand	25	— st Maclean b Calthorpe	22
C. V. Grimmett not out	18	— c and b Brand	5
P. Wallace b Tyldesley	0		
B 14, l-b 2	16	L-b	1
	278		**164**

BOWLING
VICTORIA

	Overs	Mdns	Runs	Wkts		Overs	Mdns	Runs	Wkts
Wallace	13	1	64	3	......	14	0	50	0
Keating	12	2	33	1	......	4	1	19	0
Liddicut	12	2	41	0	......	11	0	41	1
Grimmett	11	0	43	1	......	1	0	7	1
Hartkopf	6.5	0	23	5	......	20.6	2	105	8

MCC

	Overs	Mdns	Runs	Wkts		Overs	Mdns	Runs	Wkts
Gibson	23	4	58	3	......	14.4	0	61	1
Freeman	23	4	81	2	......	4	0	16	0
Tyldesley	13.3	3	25	1	......	5	0	21	2
Calthorpe	14	1	60	0	......	12	2	41	4
Chapman	1	0	5	0					
Brand	9	2	33	2	......	8	3	24	1

Lost by two wickets

153

Played at SYDNEY   **November 24, 25, 27**

MCC

Mr A. C. Wilkinson b Hendry	10	— b Kelleway	8
Mr C. H. Titchmarsh b Kelleway	79	— b Hendry	17
Hon. F. S. G. Calthorpe c Asher b Hendry	11	— b Macartney	21
Mr A. P. F. Chapman c Bardsley b Asher	100	— c Oldfield b Kelleway	24
Mr G. Wilson c Oldfield b Hendry	29	— c Macaulay b Kelleway	2
Hon. D. F. Brand b Kelleway	6	— c Asher b Hendry	4
Mr A. C. MacLaren b Hendry	54	— not out	28
Mr J. F. Maclean c Oldfield b Kelleway	33	— b Macartney	1
Mr C. H. Gibson c Collins b Kelleway	5	— c Andrews b Mailey	3
H. Tyldesley run out	0	— b Kelleway	4
A. P. Freeman not out	26	— c Hendry b Mailey	0
L-b 5, n-b 2	7	B 3, l-b 1, w 2, n-b 3	9

360   121

NEW SOUTH WALES

W. Bardsley c Wilson b Freeman	6	— b Gibson	7
H. L. Collins b Freeman	24	— lbw, b Tyldesley	22
C. G. Macartney c and b Tyldesley	63	— b Gibson	84
A. F. Kippax c Maclean b Brand	34	— b Gibson	41
T. J. Andrews b Brand	36	— lbw, b Calthorpe	74
C. Kelleway c Maclean b Tyldesley	15	— not out	32
A. Scanes b Tyldesley	3	— not out	13
H. L. Hendry run out	9		
O. P. Asher not out	6		
W. A. Oldfield c MacLaren b Brand	0		
A. A. Mailey b Brand	0		
B 1, l-b 4	5	B 7, l-b 3	10

201   283

BOWLING
NEW SOUTH WALES

	Overs	Mdns	Runs	Wkts	Overs	Mdns	Runs	Wkts
Kelleway	24.1	6	81	4	13.3	2	39	4
Hendry	20	5	64	4	11	1	48	2
Mailey	13	0	106	0	9	2	17	2
Asher	16	0	70	1				
Andrews	3	0	32	0				
Macartney	—	—	—	—	6	2	8	2

MCC

	Overs	Mdns	Runs	Wkts	Overs	Mdns	Runs	Wkts
Gibson	11	1	46	0	20.6	2	80	3
Freeman	9	0	41	2	6	1	36	0
Calthorpe	6	0	19	0	13	0	66	1
Tyldesley	15	2	47	3	13	1	67	1
Brand	9.5	0	43	4	6	1	24	0

Lost by five wickets

154

AUCKLAND v MCC

Played at AUCKLAND   December 15, 16, 18

MCC

Mr. T. C. Lowry c Rowntree b Allcott	29
Mr A. C. MacLaren st Rowntree b Anthony	58
Mr C. H. Titchmarsh b Anthony	154
Mr A. C. Wilkinson run out	50
Mr W. W. Hill-Wood c Allcott b Anthony	5
Mr A. P. F. Chapman c Dacre b Anthony	14
Hon. F. S. G. Calthorpe b Anthony	0
Mr G. Wilson c and b Anthony	5
Col. J. C. Hartley not out	16
Hon. D. F. Brand c Whelan b Smith	9
Mr C. H. Gibson c Allcott b Smith	7
L-b	3
	350

AUCKLAND

S. G. Smith b Brand	25
A. Anthony c MacLaren b Calthorpe	4
N. C. Snedden c Chapman b Brand	18
E. G. McLeod c Chapman b Brand	8
D. R. Garrard not out	37
C. C. Dacre c Hill-Wood b Brand	6
R. E. Frater not out	6
B 2, l-b 1	3
	107

A. Player
R. W. Rowntree
C. F. W. Allcott   } did not bat
J. Whelan

BOWLING
AUCKLAND

	Overs	Mdns	Runs	Wkts
Player	12	0	49	0
Allcott	31	5	103	1
Garrard	11	3	31	0
Snedden	9	2	41	0
Anthony	14	0	43	6
Smith	15.5	2	63	2
Dacre	4	1	17	0

MCC

	Overs	Mdns	Runs	Wkts
Gibson	6	2	9	0
Calthorpe	6	2	29	1
Hill-Wood	9	2	35	0
Brand	10	3	31	4
Chapman	1	1	0	0

Match drawn

MINOR ASSOCIATIONS v MCC
(N. Taranaki, S. Taranaki, Wanganui, Waikato)
Played at WANGANUI   **December 19, 20**

WANGANUI

R. G. Orr b Gibson	1 — b Calthorpe	11
R. P. London b Calthorpe	5 — c MacLaren b Gibson	13
H. N. Lambert c Hill-Wood b Brand	66 — b Gibson	63
Rev. E. O. Blamires b Gibson	5 — c Wilkinson b Gibson	31
C. A. Holland c Chapman b Hartley	16 — absent	0
H. Williams lbw, b Brand	2 — b Calthorpe	24
R. W. Orton b Brand	0 — c Maclean b Gibson	6
L. A. Wood lbw, b Gibson	8 — not out	37
H. Gilmour b Calthorpe	14 — b Brand	0
E. W. Hughes b Calthorpe	2 — c Chapman b Gibson	0
C. G. Clark not out	2 — st Maclean b Hill-Wood	2
B	8 B 12, n-b 1	13
	129	**200**

MCC

Hon. F. S. G. Calthorpe c London b Hughes	117
Mr C. H. Gibson c Gilmour b Williams	33
Mr A. C. Wilkinson c Orr b Clark	35
Hon. D. F. Brand c Hughes b Clark	30
Mr A. P. F. Chapman b Hughes	1
Mr A. C. MacLaren b Gilmour	12
Mr T. C. Lowry c Clark b Gilmour	8 — not out 38
Mr G. Wilson st Blamires b Lambert	8
Mr J. F. Maclean c sub b Gilmour	17
Mr W. W. Hill-Wood not out	11 — not out 12
Col. J. C. Hartley run out	4
B	20 B 6
	296 **56**

BOWLING
MCC

	Overs	Mdns	Runs	Wkts		Overs	Mdns	Runs	Wkts
Gibson	19.1	10	38	3		24	5	72	5
Calthorpe	15	2	42	3		19	5	48	2
Brand	8	1	30	3		10	1	51	1
Hartley	5	0	11	1		5	1	14	0
Chapman	—	—	—	—		1	1	0	0
Hill-Wood	—	—	—	—		2.2	0	2	1

WANGANUI

	Overs	Mdns	Runs	Wkts		Overs	Mdns	Runs	Wkts
Holland	7	2	18	0					
Lambert	13.3	0	65	1		4	0	16	0
Clark	16	1	83	2		3	0	22	0
Williams	9	1	46	1					
Gilmour	8	0	48	3					
Hughes	5	0	16	2		.3	0	6	0
Blamires	—	—	—	—		1	0	6	0

Won by ten wickets

156

Played at CANTERBURY   December 23, 25, 26

MCC

Mr W. W. Hill-Wood b Sandman	19	— not out	0
Mr T. C. Lowry c Brunton b Read	27	— st Hayes b Sandman	12
Mr C. H. Titchmarsh b Read	5	— c Blunt b Read	10
Mr A. C. Wilkinson c Worker b Sandman	102	— not out	1
Mr A. P. F. Chapman run out	183		
Hon. F. S. G. Calthorpe c Smith b Hayes	60		
Mr G. Wilson not out	15		
Hon. D. F. Brand not out	23		
B 14, l-b 6	20		

*454   23

Innings declared closed

CANTERBURY

R. C. Blunt c Wilson b Gibson	13	— b Gibson	174
R. V. de R. Worker c Chapman b Gibson	16	— c and b Gibson	65
F. Smith b Calthorpe	19	— b Gibson	0
W. Hayes c Lowry b Hartley	20	— b Brand	6
W. R. Patrick c Titchmarsh b Calthorpe	18	— b Gibson	0
J. Young lbw, b Hartley	0	— not out	28
D. M. Sandman st Lowry b Hartley	43	— c Wilkinson b Gibson	8
A. W. Thomas c Chapman b Hartley	2	— b Gibson	0
R. Read b Gibson	27	— b Gibson	0
C. T. Rix b Gibson	0	— b Gibson	0
L. R. Brunton not out	9	— b Brand	0
B 10, l-b 4	14	B 10, l-b 4	14

181   295

BOWLING
CANTERBURY

	Overs	Mdns	Runs	Wkts	Overs	Mdns	Runs	Wkts
Read	30	2	136	2	4	0	9	1
Rix	16	1	70	0				
Sandman	27	3	102	2	4	0	14	1
Hayes	14	4	54	1				
Thomas	13	5	23	0				
Patrick	7	0	27	0				
Blunt	5	0	22	0				

MCC

	Overs	Mdns	Runs	Wkts	Overs	Mdns	Runs	Wkts
Gibson	22	2	77	4	33	19	57	8
Calthorpe	27	14	35	2	18	6	56	0
Hartley	15.1	2	55	4	11	1	35	0
Brand	—	—	—	—	25.5	5	92	2
Hill-Wood	—	—	—	—	6	0	35	0
Chapman	—	—	—	—	2	1	6	0

Won by eight wickets

NEW ZEALAND v MCC

Played at WELLINGTON   **December 30, January 1, 2**

MCC

Mr C. H. Titchmarsh lbw, b Brice . .	22	Hon. D. F. Brand c Snedden b	
Mr A. C. Wilkinson c Collins b		Shepherd	33
Brice	17	Mr J. F. Maclean c Hiddleston b	
Hon. F. S. G. Calthorpe c Condliffe b		Snedden	84
Garrard	63	A. P. Freeman not out	0
Mr A. P. F. Chapman c Allcott b		B 17, l-b 1, n-b 1	19
Brice	1		—
Mr G. Wilson c Condliffe b Snedden	12		*505
Mr A. C. MacLaren not out 200		Mr C. H. Gibson did not bat	
Mr T. C. Lowry b Allcott	54		

Innings declared closed

NEW ZEALAND

J. S. Hiddleston c MacLaren b Gibson	5 —	c MacLaren b Gibson	38
R. C. Blunt c Chapman b Freeman	15 —	c MacLaren b Freeman	25
N. C. Snedden b Gibson	5 —	b Freeman	10
S. G. Smith run out	0 —	c Chapman b Gibson	0
J. S. Shepherd c Chapman b Freeman	33 —	b Gibson	0
D. C. Collins hit wkt., b Freeman	13 —	c Titchmarsh b Gibson	0
E. G. McLeod c Brand b Freeman	22 —	b Freeman	9
D. R. Garrard b Freeman	47 —	not out	19
C. F. W. Allcott not out	38 —	b Freeman	0
J. W. Condliffe c Lowry b Calthorpe	3 —	c and b Freeman	0
W. S. Brice c MacLaren b Calthorpe	16 —	c MacLaren b Gibson	22
B 13, l-b 12	25	B 3, l-b 1	4
	—		—
	222		127

BOWLING
NEW ZEALAND

	Overs	Mdns	Runs	Wkts
Brice	36	8	135	3
Allcott	32	4	96	1
Garrard	27	8	53	1
Smith	20	4	68	0
Snedden	11.3	1	53	2
Hiddleston	5	0	14	0
Collins	6	0	30	0
Shepherd	8	0	32	1
Blunt	3	0	5	0

MCC

	Overs	Mdns	Runs	Wkts				
Gibson	25	8	53	2	. . . . . .	33.2	19	42	5
Freeman	40	9	114	5	. . . . . .	32	13	72	5
Calthorpe	15.2	6	30	2				
Brand	—	—	—	—	. . . . . .	1	0	9	0

Won by an innings and 156 runs

158

Played at CHRISTCHURCH   January 5, 6, 8

NEW ZEALAND

D. C. Collins c and b Brand 102	— c Wilson b Calthorpe	13
R. C. Blunt c Freeman b Brand 33	— b Freeman	6
N. C. Snedden c Titchmarsh b Brand 0	— c Titchmarsh b Brand	58
H. N. Lambert b Freeman 33	— not out	47
J. S. Shepherd lbw, b Calthorpe 66	— b Calthorpe	19
D. R. Garrard c Maclean b Calthorpe 6	— b Gibson	1
C. C. Dacre c Titchmarsh b Calthorpe 45	— c Lowry b Brand	58
E. H. L. Bernau c Freeman b Calthorpe 2	— c Chapman b Freeman	34
H. M. McGirr not out 40	— c Calthorpe b Gibson	0
C. F. W. Allcott c Maclean b Gibson 16		
J. W. Condliffe lbw, b Freeman 1		
B 27, l-b 3, n-b 1 31	B 30, l-b 4	34
375	*270	

Innings declared closed

MCC

Mr G. Wilson c Shepherd b McGirr 6	— st Condliffe b Blunt	20
Mr C. H. Titchmarsh b Bernau 13	— c Blunt b Snedden	38
Mr A. C. Wilkinson b Bernau 59	— not out	41
Mr A. P. F. Chapman b Bernau 77	— c Allcott b Shepherd	3
Hon. F. S. G. Calthorpe b McGirr 14	— c Collins b Shepherd	11
Mr T. C. Lowry st Condliffe b Garrard 61	— c and b Allcott	13
Mr J. F. Maclean c McGirr b Allcott 7	— not out	8
Col. J. C. Hartley not out 60		
Hon. D. F. Brand c Collins b McGirr 22		
Mr C. H. Gibson c Allcott b Bernau 20		
A. P. Freeman c and b McGirr 14		
B 23, l-b 8 31	B 8, l-b 3	11
384	145	

BOWLING
MCC

	Overs	Mdns	Runs	Wkts	Overs	Mdns	Runs	Wkts
Gibson	25	3	89	1	23	3	86	2
Freeman	34.2	8	80	2	13.1	5	41	2
Brand	18	4	84	3	10	0	58	2
Calthorpe	22	4	78	4	14	3	51	2
Hartley	4	1	13	0				

NEW ZEALAND

	Overs	Mdns	Runs	Wkts	Overs	Mdns	Runs	Wkts
McGirr	33.5	6	96	4	9	1	26	0
Allcott	28	12	67	1	11	4	25	1
Bernau	35	10	99	4	4	0	20	0
Garrard	18	5	45	1	8	2	22	0
Snedden	10	1	25	0	4	1	8	1
Blunt	4	1	14	0	4	0	13	1
Shepherd	3	0	7	0	5	1	20	2

Match drawn

MINOR ASSOCIATIONS v MCC
(Ashburton, S. Canterbury, N. Otago)
Played at TEMUKA   **January 9, 10**

MINOR ASSOCIATIONS

W. Uttley b Chapman	0 —	c Brand b Titchmarsh	10
L. Eaton c Brand b Tyldesley	6 —	c and b Titchmarsh	20
J. B. Nicoll b Hill-Wood	15 —	b Wilson	13
J. Kane lbw, b Tyldesley	8 —	c Brand b Titchmarsh	5
C. Muff c Titchmarsh b Tyldesley	9 —	c Lowry b Chapman	14
C. Hind st Maclean b Hill-Wood	2 —	c Lowry b Wilson	0
P. W. Hargreaves st Maclean b Tyldesley	2 —	run out	20
G. Gale b Hill-Wood	0 —	c Hill-Wood b Titchmarsh	2
J. McWhirter st Maclean b Hill-Wood	4 —	c Tyldesley b Wilson	1
Rev. W. A. Hay b Tyldesley	0 —	c Calthorpe b Hartley	34
F. Jones not out	1 —	not out	12
N-b	5	B 12, l-b 3, w 1, n-b 4	20
	52		**151**

MCC

Mr J. F. Maclean c Gale b McWhirter	17
Hon. D. F. Brand c Uttley b Hargreaves	85
Mr C. H. Gibson c Jones b Hargreaves	29
Mr W. W. Hill-Wood lbw, b McWhirter	48
Mr T. C. Lowry lbw, b McWhirter	48
Col. J. C. Hartley b Hay	31
Mr A. P. F. Chapman not out	84
H. Tyldesley c Hind b Hay	17
Mr C. H. Titchmarsh b McWhirter	8
Mr G. Wilson b McWhirter	4
Hon. F. S. G. Calthorpe b McWhirter	50
B 5, l-b 3	8
	407

BOWLING
MCC

	Overs	Mdns	Runs	Wkts	Overs	Mdns	Runs	Wkts
Chapman	7	4	6	1	4	0	27	1
Tyldesley	15.3	8	19	5				
Hill-Wood	9	2	22	4				
Titchmarsh	—	—	—	—	13	1	44	4
Maclean	—	—	—	—	10	4	22	0
Wilson	—	—	—	—	11	4	17	3
Hartley	—	—	—	—	5	1	21	1

MINOR ASSOCIATIONS

McWhirter	21.5	1	153	6
Hay	16	1	87	2
Kane	7	0	57	0
Hargreaves	9	0	76	2
Muff	3	0	26	0

Won by an innings and 204 runs

Played at DUNEDIN | **January 12, 13, 15**

OTAGO

H. C. Alloo b Calthorpe	2	— b Calthorpe	0
J. S. Shepherd b Tyldesley	52	— c and b Calthorpe	9
A. W. Alloo b Calthorpe	5	— c Chapman b Freeman	19
J. McMullan b Tyldesley	8	— st Maclean b Freeman	69
A. Galland c and b Tyldesley	58	— st Maclean b Freeman	4
G. R. Dickinson c Wilkinson b Hartley	17	— lbw, b Hartley	3
H. Duncan run out	0	— c Tyldesley b Freeman	1
N. Conradi c Maclean b Freeman	39	— c Titchmarsh b Calthorpe	1
A. Knight not out	10	— c Wilkinson b Hartley	6
D. McBeath c Tyldesley b Freeman	0	— c Chapman b Hartley	0
R. Torrance b Freeman	0	— not out	7
B 4, l-b 6, n-b 1	11	B 5, l-b 5	10
	202		**129**

MCC

Mr W. W. Hill-Wood b A. W. Alloo	14	— c H. C. Alloo b McBeath	36
Mr A. C. Wilkinson c Shepherd b Dickinson	20	— c McBeath b Torrance	2
Mr C. H. Titchmarsh c McMullan b Torrance	73	— not out	37
Mr J. F. Maclean c McBeath b Torrance	24		
Mr A. P. F. Chapman c Torrance b McBeath	53	— c Duncan b McBeath	0
Mr G. Wilson b Torrance	4	— c Knight b A. W. Alloo	0
Hon. F. S. G. Calthorpe c Conradi b McBeath	0	— not out	28
Mr T. C. Lowry c Conradi b McBeath	4		
Col. J. C. Hartley not out	4		
A. P. Freeman run out	7		
H. Tyldesley c Shepherd b McBeath	15		
B	4	B 8, l-b 1	9
	222		**112**

BOWLING
MCC

	Overs	Mdns	Runs	Wkts	Overs	Mdns	Runs	Wkts
Calthorpe	23	4	65	2	14	4	28	3
Freeman	10.5	5	16	3	25.3	13	51	4
Tyldesley	22	3	72	3	3	1	8	0
Chapman	4	0	19	0				
Hartley	6	1	19	1	9	1	32	3

OTAGO

	Overs	Mdns	Runs	Wkts	Overs	Mdns	Runs	Wkts
McBeath	27.3	9	66	4	21	5	60	2
Dickinson	8	0	36	1				
A. W. Alloo	12	1	44	1	11	2	18	1
Torrance	20	6	43	3	9	1	25	1
Shepherd	5	0	27	0				
Conradi	1	0	2	0				

Won by six wickets

161

SOUTHLAND v MCC
Played at INVERCARGILL   **January 20, 22**

MCC

Mr C. H. Titchmarsh c Doig b Groves	8		
Mr G. Wilson b Fogo	42		
Mr A. C. Wilkinson c Doig b Fogo	33		
Hon. F. S. G. Calthorpe c Poole b Fogo	77		
Mr J. F. Maclean c Kavanagh b Fogo	25 —	not out	12
Col. J. C. Hartley c Groves b Kavanagh	15 —	not out	9
Hon. D. F. Brand c Hamilton b Kavanagh .	25 —	st Gilbertson b Kavanagh ...	23
Mr C. H. Gibson not out	39 —	b Kavanagh	7
A. P. Freeman c Kavanagh b Doig	49 —	c Fogo b Kavanagh	7
Mr B. S. Hill-Wood run out	2 —	c and b Groves	0
H. Tyldesley c Glozier b Poole	0 —	c Dixon b Fogo	40
B 3, l-b 1	4	B	3
	319		***101**

*Innings declared closed

SOUTHLAND

E. Kavanagh b Calthorpe	8 —	c Calthorpe b Hartley	15
A. Hamilton c Calthorpe b Tyldesley	1 —	c Calthorpe b Freeman	2
A. Poole b Hartley	46 —	c Wilkinson b Gibson	0
T. Groves c Tyldesley b Hartley	32 —	b Calthorpe	11
J. Hamilton c Tyldesley b Hartley	0 —	b Calthorpe	2
A. Driscoll lbw, b Brand	10 —	b Calthorpe	1
J. Gilbertson not out	15 —	lbw, b Calthorpe	8
J. A. Doig c Gibson b Brand	1 —	not out	13
C. Dixon c Freeman b Tyldesley	7 —	b Calthorpe	0
A. Glozier c Tyldesley b Calthorpe	17 —	b Hartley	4
R. Fogo c Wilson b Gibson	3 —	b B. S. Hill-Wood	0
B 11, l-b 2	13	B 8, l-b 6, n-b 1	15
	153		**71**

BOWLING
SOUTHLAND

	Overs	Mdns	Runs	Wkts	Overs	Mdns	Runs	Wkts
Groves	10	0	55	1	3	0	12	1
Doig	17	4	40	1	2	0	11	0
Fogo	24	4	99	4	8	1	33	1
Kavanagh	14	2	71	2	9	1	42	3
Glozier	6	0	28	0				
Poole	11.2	2	22	1				

MCC

	Overs	Mdns	Runs	Wkts	Overs	Mdns	Runs	Wkts
Calthorpe	12	2	24	2	12	7	17	5
Tyldesley	12	5	25	2				
Freeman	7	0	33	0	6	4	8	1
Gibson	7.4	0	34	1	8	5	5	1
Brand	6	2	13	2	3	2	2	0
Hartley	6	0	11	3	7	2	12	2
Wilkinson	—	—	—	—	1	0	12	0
B. S. Hill-Wood	—	—	—	—	0.5	0	0	1

Won by 196 runs

Played at WELLINGTON   **January 26, 27, 29**

WELLINGTON

J. S. Hiddleston c Maclean b Calthorpe	38	— b Calthorpe	17
D. C. Collins, hit wkt., b Calthorpe	7	— c Calthorpe b Brand	2
E. H. L. Bernau c and b Gibson	4	— c Chapman b Calthorpe	19
B. J. Kortlang c and b Gibson	0	— b Gibson	9
W. A. Baker b Brand	35	— c Maclean b Gibson	0
H. M. McGirr c Chapman b Calthorpe	0	— st Maclean b Freeman	7
C. S. Dempster lbw, b Gibson	3	— run out	36
W. S. Brice run out	0	— run out	0
C. W. Grant b Calthorpe	12	— b Brand	7
H. J. Tattersall not out	4	— c Brand b Freeman	17
M. Henderson st Maclean b Brand	0	— not out	8
N-b	1	B 7, l-b 2, n-b 2	11
	104		**133**

MCC

Mr A. C. Wilkinson lbw, b Brice	0	— b Brice	1
Mr C. H. Titchmarsh c Brice b Bernau	21	— b Brice	64
Mr T. C. Lowry c Dempster b Bernau	15	— b Brice	3
Mr A. P. F. Chapman c Kortlang b McGirr	18	— b Brice	5
Hon. F. S. G. Calthorpe b Brice	0	— b Brice	0
Mr W. W. Hill-Wood b Brice	4	— c Grant b Henderson	21
Mr J. F. Maclean c Hiddleston b McGirr ...	29	— not out	11
Col. J. C. Hartley b Brice	2	— not out	4
Hon. D. F. Brand c Hiddleston b McGirr ..	1		
Mr C. H. Gibson b Brice	15		
A. P. Freeman not out	2		
		B 20, l-b 1, n-b 1	22
	107		**131**

BOWLING
MCC

	Overs	Mdns	Runs	Wkts	Overs	Mdns	Runs	Wkts
Gibson	25	9	59	3	16	7	23	2
Calthorpe	26	13	44	4	18	4	38	2
Brand	1.2	1	0	2	10	1	32	2
Freeman	—	—	—	—	9	2	29	2

WELLINGTON

	Overs	Mdns	Runs	Wkts	Overs	Mdns	Runs	Wkts
Brice	15	2	52	5	20	6	45	5
Bernau	9	1	32	2	6	1	11	0
McGirr	5	1	23	3	10	3	17	0
Henderson	—	—	—	—	8	2	18	1
Grant	—	—	—	—	2	1	5	0
Hiddleston	—	—	—	—	3	0	6	0
Collins	—	—	—	—	1	0	7	0

Won by four wickets

163

Played at NELSON   **January 30, 31**

MINOR ASSOCIATIONS

K. R. Saxon c Wilkinson b Freeman	60	—	c W. W. Hill-Wood b B. S. Hill-Wood	1
E. R. Neale c and b Tyldesley	3	—	b Brand	0
S. Hincksman c Chapman b B. S. Hill-Wood	0	—	st Lowry b Freeman	6
A. H. McKellar c Slater b B. S. Hill-Wood	0	—	b Freeman	10
R. J. Pearpoint c Wilkinson b Tyldesley	4	—	c and b Freeman	0
M. O. Eden c Maclean b Tyldesley	0	—	b Freeman	3
E. J. Kemnitz c Chapman b B. S. Hill-Wood	18	—	c Tyldesley b Brand	22
E. Reid run out	6	—	b Brand	1
T. B. Louisson c Tyldesley b Freeman	9	—	c Chapman b Freeman	0
J. Newman b Brand	3	—	not out	2
H. Fass not out	0	—	lbw, b Freeman	3
B 10, l-b 1, n-b 5	16		B 4, l-b 2, n-b 1	7
	119			**55**

MCC

Mr W. W. Hill-Wood b Newman	16	A. P. Freeman b Newman	13
Hon. D. F. Brand b Louisson	0	Mr B. S. Hill-Wood lbw, b Louisson	19
Mr A. C. Wilkinson c and b McKellar	52	H. Tyldesley c McKellar b Louisson	0
Mr T. C. Lowry c Saxon b Newman	40	Mr H. D. Swan b Louisson	0
Mr A. P. F. Chapman not out	71	B 24, l-b 8	32
Mr J. F. Maclean b Newman	5		
Mr P. H. Slater b Newman	1		**249**

BOWLING
MCC

	Overs	Mdns	Runs	Wkts		Overs	Mdns	Runs	Wkts
B. S. Hill-Wood	22	7	47	3	......	8	2	16	1
Tyldesley	21	7	42	3					
Freeman	4	1	10	2	......	10.5	1	27	6
Brand	3.1	2	4	1	......	3	1	5	3

MINOR ASSOCIATIONS

	Overs	Mdns	Runs	Wkts
Louisson	20.5	6	48	4
Newman	29	5	93	5
Fass	3	0	27	0
McKellar	4	1	10	1
Neale	4	0	27	0
Reid	5	1	12	0

Won by an innings and 75 runs

NEW ZEALAND v MCC

Played at WELLINGTON   **February 2, 3, 5**

NEW ZEALAND

D. C. Collins c Chapman b Calthorpe	1	— c Maclean b Gibson	69
R. C. Blunt c Maclean b Gibson	0	— c Freeman b Gibson	68
J. S. Shepherd st Maclean b Gibson	41	— c and b Freeman	0
C. C. Dacre run out	4	— c Maclean b Freeman	17
H. N. Lambert c Freeman b Calthorpe	23	— c Wilkinson b Brand	11
D. R. Garrard b Calthorpe	19	— lbw, b Gibson	12
H. M. McGirr c Titchmarsh b Calthorpe	1	— c Chapman b Freeman	8
E. H. L. Bernau c Maclean b Calthorpe	61	— c Chapman b Freeman	3
W. S. Brice c Lowry b Gibson	10	— c Wilson b Gibson	10
A. Cate b Calthorpe	0	— lbw, b Gibson	2
D. J. McBeath not out	0	— not out	4
B 3, l-b 3	6	B 9, l-b 1, w 1	11
	166		**215**

MCC

Mr G. Wilson b Bernau	19
Mr C. H. Titchmarsh c Brice b Bernau	40
Mr A. C. Wilkinson b Bernau	27
Mr A. P. F. Chapman b McGirr	71
Mr T. C. Lowry c Dacre b McBeath	130
Hon. F. S. G. Calthorpe b Brice	0
Mr J. F. Maclean c Garrard b Collins	53
Col. J. C. Hartley c Blunt b McBeath	16
Hon. D. F. Brand b Brice	9
Mr C. H. Gibson c Lambert b McBeath	5
A. P. Freeman not out	0
B 25, l-b 5, w 1	31
	401

BOWLING
MCC

	Overs	Mdns	Runs	Wkts	Overs	Mdns	Runs	Wkts
Gibson	22	2	91	3	32.4	12	65	5
Calthorpe	21.2	6	53	6	8	4	13	0
Freeman	2	0	11	0	40	13	95	4
Brand	2	1	5	0	11	3	31	1

NEW ZEALAND

	Overs	Mdns	Runs	Wkts
Brice	33	9	75	2
McBeath	27	6	81	3
McGirr	20	1	70	1
Garrard	13	2	32	0
Bernau	20	1	68	3
Lambert	2	0	9	0
Blunt	1	0	4	0
Shepherd	4	0	25	0
Collins	1	0	6	1

Won by an innings and 20 runs

MINOR ASSOCIATIONS v MCC
(Manawatu, Rangitikei, Wairarapa)
Played at PALMERSTON NORTH   **February 6, 7**

MCC

A. P. Freeman c Bennett b Grant	3	— c Hoar b Bennett	0
Hon. F. S. G. Calthorpe c Hoar b Bennett	136		
Hon. D. F. Brand b Grant	24		
Mr A. C. Wilkinson b Hodder	6	— b Massey	2
H. Tyldesley b Massey	11	— b Massey	2
Mr W. W. Hill-Wood c Grant b Hodder	1	— c Rose b Massey	36
Col. J. C. Hartley b Grant	43		
Mr C. H. Gibson not out	58	— b Bennett	0
Mr J. F. Maclean b Bennett	3	— not out	1
Mr G. Wilson not out	11	— c Bennett b Massey	7
B 4, l-b 3, n-b 3	10	L-b	5
	*306		*53

Innings declared closed

MINOR ASSOCIATIONS

W. Eyre b Tyldesley	13	— c Freeman b W. W. Hill-Wood	20
D. Cameron b W. W. Hill-Wood	5	— st Maclean b Freeman	6
A. M. Rose b Calthorpe	30	— b Freeman	11
K. Hodder b W. W. Hill-Wood	0	— b Tyldesley	4
A. Grant c Hartley b Tyldesley	0	— b W. W. Hill-Wood	12
A. C. McVicar c Hartley b Brand	25	— b Wilkinson	10
A. Hoar b Freeman	17	— c Tyldesley b W. W. Hill-Wood	4
R. McKay b Brand	2	— c Freeman b Wilkinson	5
F. Hoar c Freeman b Brand	1	— c Hartley b Wilkinson	19
W. Bennett c Maclean b Freeman	19	— b Hartley	1
B. Massey not out	2	— not out	0
B 7, l-b 2	9	B 1, l-b 2, n-b 1	4
	123		96

BOWLING
MINOR ASSOCIATIONS

	Overs	Mdns	Runs	Wkts	Overs	Mdns	Runs	Wkts
Grant	25	4	62	3				
Bennett	18	3	83	2	11.1	3	34	2
McVicar	7	0	41	0				
Rose	3	0	14	0				
Hoar	4	0	20	0				
Hodder	8	0	52	2				
Massey	7	0	24	1	11	4	14	4

MCC

	Overs	Mdns	Runs	Wkts	Overs	Mdns	Runs	Wkts
W. W. Hill-Wood	7	2	12	2	6	0	20	3
Tyldesley	7	4	14	2	6	3	7	1
Calthorpe	6	1	21	1	6	1	17	0
Hartley	6	2	24	0	5	2	11	1
Brand	6	1	13	3				
Freeman	6	7	30	2	6	1	21	2
Wilkinson	—	—	—	—	4.5	0	16	3

Won by 140 runs

MINOR ASSOCIATIONS v MCC
(Hawke's Bay, Poverty Bay, Wairoa)
Played at NAPIER   **February 9, 10**

MCC

Mr. C. H. Titchmarsh b Bernau 30	— not out 63
Mr G. Wilson c O'Brien b Jacobsen 5	
Mr A. C. Wilkinson c Graham b	
Temperton......................... 26	— c Brown b Bernau 5
Mr A. P. F. Chapman st Ellis b	
Temperton......................... 0	— b Bernau................ 4
Hon. F. S. G. Calthorpe c McMahon b	
Temperton......................... 35	— b Temperton 28
Mr W. W. Hill-Wood c Jacobsen b Blair ... 9	— c Blair b Bernau 31
Mr J. F. Maclean b Blair 4	— not out 5
Mr C. H. Gibson c Ellis b Temperton 3	
Mr P. H. Slater b Bernau 18	
H. Tyldesley not out 7	
Mr B. S. Hill-Wood c Brown b Temperton . 3	
	B 24, l-b 3 27
140	*163

Innings declared closed

EAST COAST ASSOCIATIONS

A. C. Temperton run out 1	— not out 11
J. J. O'Brien c Calthorpe b Gibson 0	— c Maclean b Calthorpe 11
C. Brown c Maclean b Gibson 3	
E. H. L. Bernau c Calthorpe b Gibson 3	— c Maclean b Calthorpe 8
W. Blair c Gibson b Calthorpe 15	— not out 34
N. R. Jacobsen c W. W. Hill-Wood b	
Gibson 0	
L. McMahon c Wilkinson b Gibson 6	
H. Smith b Tyldesley 14	— c Slater b B. S. Hill-Wood .. 12
H. F. Forster c Calthorpe b Gibson 6	
H. Ellis not out 9	— c W. W. Hill-Wood b
	Tyldesley 54
W. Graham b Tyldesley 4	
B 5, l-b 2......................... 7	B 4, l-b 3 7
68	137

BOWLING
EAST COAST ASSOCIATIONS

	Overs	Mdns	Runs	Wkts	Overs	Mdns	Runs	Wkts
Bernau	16	6	34	2	15	0	62	3
Jacobsen	5	0	27	1	4	0	22	0
Temperton	23	6	48	5	6	1	28	1
Graham...........	3	0	17	0	9	0	24	0
Blair	9	3	14	2				

MCC

	Overs	Mdns	Runs	Wkts	Overs	Mdns	Runs	Wkts
Gibson...........	17	7	28	6	15	1	48	0
Calthorpe	16	7	28	1	15	4	37	2
Tyldesley	1	0	5	2	11	2	20	1
B. S. Hill-Wood	—	—	—	—	6	1	16	1
Chapman	—	—	—	—	2	0	2	0
Wilson	—	—	—	—	2	1	7	0

Match drawn

AUCKLAND v MCC

Played at AUCKLAND   **February 17, 19**

MCC

Mr C. H. Titchmarsh c Rowntree b Allcott 73	Col. J. C. Hartley b Anthony 15
Mr W. W. Hill-Wood lbw, b Player . 52	Hon. D. F. Brand lbw, b Allcott 1
Hon. F. S. G. Calthorpe b Allcott ... 78	Mr C. H. Gibson not out 4
Mr A. P. F. Chapman b Allcott 108	A. P. Freeman b Allcott 0
Mr T. C. Lowry b Smith 7	B 7, l-b 2 9
Mr G. Wilson b Player 10	—
Mr J. F. Maclean c McLeod b Allcott 8	**365**

AUCKLAND

R. Frater c Gibson b Freeman 26	— b Freeman 1
E. Horspool lbw, b Freeman 28	— lbw, b Freeman 0
N. C. Snedden b Freeman 31	— b Freeman 0
S. G. Smith lbw, b Gibson 5	— c Brand b Freeman 0
C. C. Dacre lbw, b Gibson 0	— c Lowry b Gibson 30
D. R. Garrard c and b Freeman 0	— b Freeman 7
A. Anthony b Gibson 6	— c Titchmarsh b Hartley 48
E. G. McLeod not out 14	— b Brand 50
C. F. W. Allcott c Hartley b Freeman 12	— not out 4
A. Player c Lowry b Freeman 18	— b Gibson 31
R. W. Rowntree c Chapman b Freeman 36	— b Gibson 1
B 2	B 10, n-b 1 11
178	**183**

BOWLING
AUCKLAND

	Overs	Mdns	Runs	Wkts
Allcott	31	4	86	6
Player	28	7	91	2
Smith	16	1	59	1
Garrard	8	0	38	0
Anthony	15	4	54	1
Snedden	6	0	28	0
Horspool	1	1	0	0

MCC

	Overs	Mdns	Runs	Wkts				
Gibson	26	6	70	3	 19	3	53	3
Calthorpe	4	1	19	0	 4	0	13	0
Freeman	22	4	87	7	 19	4	71	5
Brand	—	—	—	—	 8	1	25	1
Hartley	—	—	—	—	 3	0	10	1

Won by an innings and four runs

168

NEW SOUTH WALES v MCC

MCC

Mr C. H. Titchmarsh retired hurt	2 —	lbw, b Mailey	36
Mr W. W. Hill-Wood c Oldfield b Scott	18 —	c Oldfield b Scott	46
Hon. F. S. G. Calthorpe c Mailey b Scott	0 —	b Hendry	110
Mr A. P. F. Chapman b Andrews	91 —	c Hendry b Mailey	18
Mr T. C. Lowry c Kippax b Mailey	10 —	c Oldfield b Mailey	0
Mr G. Wilson c Oldfield b Scott	33 —	b Scott	0
Mr J. F. Maclean b Scott	6 —	c Kelleway b Mailey	0
Col. J. C. Hartley lbw, b Kelleway	48 —	c Hendry b Mailey	4
Hon. D. F. Brand c Andrews b Mailey	60 —	lbw, b Andrews	22
Mr C. H. Gibson not out	4 —	not out	30
A. P. Freeman c Taylor b Mailey	1 —	lbw, b Andrews	22
L-b 1, w 1	2	B 1, w 3, n-b 4	8
	275		**296**

NEW SOUTH WALES

H. L. Collins c Calthorpe b Gibson	10 —	b Freeman	6
W. Bardsley lbw, b Freeman	90 —	c Maclean b Gibson	26
C. G. Macartney c Chapman b Gibson	18 —	b Freeman	0
T. J. Andrews c Chapman b Gibson	37 —	st Maclean b Freeman	8
J. M. Taylor c Hill-Wood b Gibson	73 —	c Gibson b Chapman	52
A. Kippax not out	59 —	not out	6
C. Kelleway lbw, b Gibson	0		
H. L. Hendry c Gibson b Freeman	13		
W. A. Oldfield st Maclean b Freeman	0		
J. D. Scott c Chapman b Gibson	4		
A. A. Mailey b Freeman	0		
B 6, l-b 3, w 1	10	B	4
	314		**102**

BOWLING
NEW SOUTH WALES

	Overs	Mdns	Runs	Wkts	Overs	Mdns	Runs	Wkts
Scott	19	11	68	4	21	1	76	2
Kelleway	21	5	53	1	14	1	42	0
Mailey	16.1	0	91	3	29	1	118	5
Hendry	3	0	21	0	6	1	34	1
Andrews	7	0	40	1	3.7	0	18	2
Macartney	2	2	0	0				

MCC

	Overs	Mdns	Runs	Wkts	Overs	Mdns	Runs	Wkts
Gibson	32	1	140	6	12	1	42	1
Freeman	23	2	99	4	10	1	34	3
Brand	5	0	28	0				
Calthorpe	8	0	37	0				
Chapman	—	—	—	—	2.7	0	10	1
Hill-Wood	—	—	—	—	1	0	12	0

Match drawn

COMBINED UNIVERSITIES v MCC
Played at MELBOURNE   March 7, 8

MCC

Mr W. W. Hill-Wood c Rock b Jorgensen .. 84	— b Nothling 18
Mr C. H. Titchmarsh b Fisher 2	
Hon. F. S. G. Calthorpe c Bailey b Fisher .. 10	— c Bailey b Fisher 15
Mr A. P. F. Chapman b Fisher 29	— not out 29
Mr T. C. Lowry c Garner b Nothling 30	— c Rock b Freemantle 17
Mr G. Wilson b Nothling 0	— not out 13
Mr J. F. Maclean c Fisher b Nothling 13	— c Taylor b Freemantle 36
Col. J. C. Hartley c Jorgensen b Fisher 30	
Hon. D. F. Brand c Taylor b Fisher 38	
Mr C. H. Gibson c Taylor b Fisher 17	— c Taylor b Nothling 7
H. Tyldesley not out 0	
B 2, l-b 2, n-b 1 5	
258	**135**

COMBINED UNIVERSITIES

L. F. Freemantle (Melbourne) c
     Calthorpe b Brand 59
H. O. Rock (Sydney) c Brand b
     Calthorpe 35
J. M. Taylor (Sydney) b Brand 37
J. V. Garner (Sydney) b Tyldesley .. 1
W. H. Bailey (Melbourne) c Hartley
     b Calthorpe 51
L. T. Gun (S. Australia) c Tyldesley
     b Gibson 28
O. E. Nothling (Sydney) b
     Chapman 56

W. M. Irvine (Melbourne) b
     Hill-Wood 23
T. R. Street (Sydney) c Wilson b
     Chapman 18
H. W. Fisher (Adelaide) b
     Tyldesley 15
E. Jorgensen (Melbourne) not out .. 5
     B 4
         332

BOWLING
COMBINED UNIVERSITIES

	Overs	Mdns	Runs	Wkts		Overs	Mdns	Runs	Wkts
Fisher	19	1	68	6	......	7	0	35	1
Nothling	20	3	73	3	......	7	0	44	2
Jorgensen	12	0	49	1	......	2	0	5	0
Freemantle	14	0	63	0	......	4	0	17	2
Bailey	—	—	—	—	......	5	0	28	0
Gun	—	—	—	—	......	1	0	6	0

MCC

	Overs	Mdns	Runs	Wkts
Gibson	19	2	68	1
Calthorpe	18	4	73	2
Brand	13	2	61	2
Tyldesley	14	3	50	2
Hartley	3	0	25	0
Chapman	4.6	0	21	2
Hill-Wood	3	0	30	1

Match drawn

170

VICTORIA v MCC

Played at MELBOURNE   **March 9, 10, 12**

MCC

Mr W. W. Hill-Wood c Ryder b Wallace	10	— not out	122
Mr C. H. Titchmarsh c Ryder b Liddicutt	1		
Hon. F. S. G. Calthorpe b Wallace	20		
Mr A. P. F. Chapman c Ryder b Liddicutt	6		
Mr T. C. Lowry c Woodfull b Liddicutt	5		
Mr G. Wilson c Ellis b Wallace	16	— not out	142
Mr J. F. Maclean c Woodfull b Liddicutt	0		
Col. J. C. Hartley lbw, b Wallace	3		
Hon. D. F. Brand c Ryder b Wallace	2		
Mr C. H. Gibson not out	3		
A. P. Freeman c Ryder b Wallace	0		
L-b 3, w 2	5	B 11, l-b 1, w 2, n-b 4	18
	71		**282**

VICTORIA

W. M. Woodfull c Chapman b Gibson	6	W. H. Bailey not out	11
H. S. Love b Chapman	192	B 7, l-b 7	14
W. H. Ponsford st Maclean b Brand	62		
J. Ryder run out	11		***617**
R. L. Park c Wilson b Calthorpe	101	P. Wallace ⎫	
V. S. Ransford not out	118	J. Ryder ⎬ did not bat	
A. E. Liddicut c Hill-Wood b Wilson	102	T. Carlton ⎭	

Innings declared closed

BOWLING
VICTORIA

	Overs	Mdns	Runs	Wkts	Overs	Mdns	Runs	Wkts
Wallace	15.5	1	50	6	18	4	54	0
Liddicut	15	5	16	4	19	9	44	0
Ryder	—	—	—	—	11	2	36	0
Carlton	—	—	—	—	16	2	51	0
Bailey	—	—	—	—	6	0	25	0
Ransford	—	—	—	—	9	2	34	0
Love	—	—	—	—	2	0	19	0
Park	—	—	—	—	4	3	1	0

MCC

	Overs	Mdns	Runs	Wkts
Gibson	42	4	151	1
Calthorpe	18	1	90	1
Freeman	33	4	121	0
Brand	20	0	108	1
Chapman	9	0	36	1
Wilson	7	0	44	1
Hill-Wood	9	1	53	0

Match drawn

Played at ADELAIDE   **March 15, 16, 17**

SOUTH AUSTRALIA

A. Richardson c Lowry b Chapman	280		
V. Richardson run out	1		
Dr. C. Dolling b Calthorpe	10	lbw, b Gibson	33
J. T. Murray c and b Freeman	8	not out	36
C. E. Pellew c Maclean b Freeman	26	c Chapman b Freeman	69
L. Bowley run out	76	c Lowry b Freeman	35
G. W. Harris c Hill-Wood b Freeman	4	c Hill-Wood b Gibson	27
J. W. Rymill st Maclean b Freeman	50		
H. M. Fisher c and b Freeman	22		
E. J. Carragher st Maclean b Freeman	11		
A. Ambler not out	0		
B 2, l-b 5	7	B	4
	495		***204**

Innings declared closed

MCC

Mr W. W. Hill-Wood c Ambler b A. Richardson	3	b Murray	41
Mr G. Wilson st Ambler b Murray	78	not out	6
Hon. F. S. G. Calthorpe c A. Richardson b Carragher	96	b Murray	12
Mr A. P. F. Chapman b Fisher	49	not out	134
Mr T. C. Lowry b Bowley	17	b Carragher	45
Mr C. H. Titchmarsh b Fisher	0	lbw, b Fisher	5
Mr J. F. Maclean c and b Fisher	37		
Col. J. C. Hartley not out	28		
Hon. D. F. Brand b Fisher	0		
Mr C. H. Gibson b Fisher	0		
A. P. Freeman c Fisher b Carragher	57		
B1, l-b 6	7	B 3, l-b 2	5
	372		**248**

BOWLING
MCC

	Overs	Mdns	Runs	Wkts		Overs	Mdns	Runs	Wkts
Gibson	27	3	127	0		15.2	1	87	2
Freeman	27.7	0	176	6		12	0	92	2
Calthorpe	11	0	101	1		3	0	21	0
Brand	3	0	51	0					
Chapman	6	0	33	1					

SOUTH AUSTRALIA

	Overs	Mdns	Runs	Wkts		Overs	Mdns	Runs	Wkts
Fisher	20	0	96	5		8	0	59	1
A. Richardson	21	4	60	1					
Carragher	18.7	1	123	2		7	0	69	1
Bowley	7	1	52	1		4	0	33	0
Murray	5	0	27	1		10	0	63	2
Pellew	2	0	7	0		3	0	19	0

Match drawn

MCC BATTING AVERAGES

	Innings	Runs	Highest inns	Not outs	Average
Mr A. P. F. Chapman	31	.. 1533	.. 183	.. 4	.. 56.77
Mr C. H. Titchmarsh	30	.. 998	.. 154	.. 4	.. 38.38
Hon. F. S. G. Calthorpe ..	30	.. 1038	.. 136	.. 1	.. 35.79
Mr W. W. Hill-Wood	28	.. 699	.. 122*	.. 4	.. 29.12
Mr A. C. Wilkinson	26	.. 689	.. 102	.. 2	.. 28.70
Col J. C. Hartley	18	.. 335	.. 60*	.. 6	.. 27.91
Mr T. C. Lowry	25	.. 654	.. 130	.. 1	.. 27.25
Mr G. Wilson	29	.. 598	.. 142*	.. 5	.. 24.91
Mr J. F. Maclean	27	.. 458	.. 84	.. 6	.. 21.80
Hon. D. F. Brand	24	.. 469	.. 85	.. 2	.. 21.31
Mr C. H. Gibson	25	.. 326	.. 58*	.. 7	.. 18.12
A. P. Freeman	21	.. 202	.. 57	.. 7	.. 14.42
H. Tyldesley	16	.. 116	.. 40	.. 2	.. 8.28

The following also batted:— Mr A. C. MacLaren, 9—410—200*—2—58.57; Mr B. S. Hill-Wood, 2, 0, 19 and 3; Mr H. D. Swan, 0 and 0; Mr P. H. Slater, 1 and 18.

Signifies not out

MCC BOWLING AVERAGES

	Overs	Maidens	Runs	Wickets	Average
Col. J. C. Hartley	90.1	.. 14	.. 293	.. 17	.. 17.23
H. Tyldesley	194.3	.. 45	.. 581	.. 33	.. 17.60
Hon. D. F. Brand	219	.. 39	.. 881	.. 41	.. 21.48
A. P. Freeman	502.1	.. 109	.. 1785	.. 82	.. 21.76
Mr C. H. Gibson	663.1	.. 153	.. 1980	.. 79	.. 25.06
Hon. F. S. G. Calthorpe ..	435	.. 109	.. 1369	.. 54	.. 25.35

The following also bowled:—Mr W. W. Hill-Wood, 55—7—251—11; Mr A. P. F. Chapman, 46.5—7—180—7; Mr B. S. Hill-Wood, 36.5—10—79—6; Mr G. Wilson, 20—5—68—4.

──•BIBLIOGRAPHY•──

BOOKS (Place of publication is London unless otherwise stated)

Anderson, W. P., *Cricket in the Palmerston North Boys' High School, 1902-1946*, Palmerston North, 1946.

Brittenden, R. T., *Great Days in New Zealand Cricket*, Bailey Bros & Swinfen, Wellington, 1958.

Brittenden, R. T., *New Zealand Cricketers*, A. H. & A. W. Reed, Wellington, 1961.

Brittenden, R. T., *100 Years of Cricket: A History of the Canterbury Cricket Association, 1877-1977*, Christchurch, c.1978.

Butler, Samuel, *A First Year in Canterbury Settlement*, A. C. Fifield, 1914.

Cane, F. F., *Cricket Centenary: the story of cricket in Hawke's Bay, 1855-1955*, Napier, 1959.

Carman, Arthur H., *New Zealand International Cricket, 1894-1974*, A. H. & A. W. Reed, Wellington, 1975.

Carman, Arthur H., *Wellington Cricket Centenary, 1875-1975*, Sporting Publications, Tawa, 1975.

Down, Michael, *Archie: A Biography of A. C. MacLaren*, George Allen & Unwin, 1981.

Ferguson, W. H., *Mr Cricket*, Kaye, 1957.

Gibson, Alan, *The Cricket Captains of England*, Cassell, 1979.

Hintz, O. S., *The New Zealanders in England, 1931*, J. M. Dent, 1931.

Lemmon, David, *'Tich' Freeman and the Decline of the Leg-Break Bowler*, George Allen & Uwin, 1982.

MacLaren, A. C., *Cricket Old and New*, Longmans, Green, 1924.

Martin-Jenkins, Christopher, *The Complete Who's Who of Test Cricketers*, Orbis, revised edition, 1983.

May, P. R., *With the MCC in New Zealand*, Eyre & Spottiswoode, 1907.

Mitchell, Alan, *84 Not Out: the story of Sir Arthur Sims*, Locke, 1962.

Murry, J. Middleton (ed.), *Journal of Katherine Mansfield*, Constable, 1954.

Neely, Don, *100 Summers: The History of Wellington Cricket*, Wellington, 1975.

Otago Cricket Association, *Centennial Souvenir Programme, 1876-1976*, Dunedin, 1976.

Reese, Daniel, *Was It All Cricket?*, George Allen & Unwin, 1948.

Reese, T. W., *New Zealand Cricket, 1841-1914*, Simpson & Williams, Christchurch, 1927.

Reese, T. W., *New Zealand Cricket, 1914-1933*, Whitcombe & Tombs, Christchurch, 1936.

Shaw, Alfred, *Alfred Shaw, Cricketer*, Cassell, 1902.
Swanton, E.W. (ed.), *Barclays World of Cricket*, Collins, 1980.
Turnbull, M.J., and Allom M.J.C., *The Book of the Two Maurices*, E.Allom, 1930.
Warner, P.F., *Cricket Across The Seas*, Longmans, 1903.

NEWSPAPERS
Outside New Zealand:
Advertiser (Adelaide)
Argus (Melbourne)
Australasian (Melbourne)
Ceylon Observer
Daily Telegraph (Sydney)
Leader (Melbourne)
Referee (Sydney)
Register (Adelaide)
Sydney Morning Herald
Times of Ceylon
West Australian (Perth)

New Zealand:
Auckland:
Auckland Star, Auckland Weekly News, New Zealand Herald, New Zealand Illustrated Sporting and Dramatic Review, New Zealand Observer

Christchurch:
Lyttelton Times, Press, Sun, Weekly Press

Dunedin:
Daily Telegraph, Evening Star, Otago Daily Times, Otago Witness

Invercargill:
Southland Daily News, Southland Times

Napier:
Daily Telegraph, Hawke's Bay Herald

Nelson:
Nelson Evening Mail

Palmerston North:
Manawatu Evening Standard

South Canterbury:
Temuka Leader, Timaru Herald, Timaru Post

Wanganui:
Wanganui Chronicle, Wanganui Herald

Wellington:
Dominion, Evening Post, New Zealand Free Lance, New Zealand Mail, New Zealand Times

'MacLaren's cricket belonged to the golden age of the game, to the spacious and opulent England of his day; it knew not the common touch. He spent the later years of his life incessantly urging modern players to return to first principles, to the classical batting action, with the left shoulder forward, to the free pick-up of the bat, and to the rhythmical swing through, "body into the shot".'

Manchester Guardian obituary

'It might fairly be said that Archie was not quite the same to all men, but all the members of our team were devoted to him. We were enthralled by his superb technique and his shrewd leadership, but there may have been times when he was a little awkward.'

Alex Wilkinson

'Borrowed five pounds from me once to pay his champagne account, and I am still waiting for it to be returned.'

W. H. Ferguson